THE POSSIBILITY OF
RELIGIOUS KNOWLEDGE

The Possibility of Religious Knowledge

by

JERRY H. GILL
Associate Professor of Philosophy
Florida Presbyterian College

WILLIAM B. EERDMANS PUBLISHING COMPANY
GRAND RAPIDS, MICHIGAN

Dedicated

to

Ian Thomas Ramsey

Preface

How is religious knowledge possible? This is the question that has dominated my thought for some ten years. As one who is both a Christian and a philosopher, I have continuously wrestled with the issues raised by the interaction between these two commitments. On the one hand I find religious knowledge not only a possibility, but an obvious actuality in my daily life. On the other hand I find it necessary to ask continuously for a rational account of such a possibility. Rather than alleviate the tension created by this dual commitment by jettisoning one or the other, I have sought to bring them into a functional relationship. My results are presented on the following pages.

In my efforts to justify a belief in the possibility of religious knowledge I have become convinced that in our day the chief obstacle to such a justification is the epistemological dualism underlying all modern thought. Thus in Part One of my study I have sought to document this dualism, together with its effects, in twentieth-century philosophy and theology, and I have also traced its roots back through the nineteenth century to the philosophy of Immanuel Kant. In Part Two I have drawn heavily on the work of Ludwig Wittgenstein, J. L. Austin, and their followers in establishing a functional view of language to serve as a point of departure from which to reconstruct modern epistemology. My conclusion, based upon the main emphases of Michael Polanyi, is that the knowing experience is best understood as composed of dimensional and contextual awareness, together with committed and functional response. The interaction between these two aspects of the knowing experience calls attention to the tacit and mediated aspects of knowledge as well as to its more direct and explicit aspects. In Part Three I have concluded that the concept of tacit knowledge makes it possible to speak of religious knowledge as discerned in mediated revelation and approximated in properly qualified theological language. In arriving at these conclusions, I have drawn heavily on the work of John Hick, John Wisdom, and Ian Ramsey.

The question of whether or not religious knowledge is possible must be distinguished from the question of whether or not it is actual. This book seeks to establish the claim that such knowledge is a possibility, but it does not go far toward showing that it is an actuality. In the last analysis the question of the actuality of religious knowledge can be answered only by each individual. Given the understanding of cognitive experience set forth in the following chapters, each individual must examine his own experience for the sort of discernment and response that characterizes religious knowing. Hopefully the concepts and categories I have presented will make it possible for some persons to become aware in their own lives of the religious dimension. In addition some who are already religiously aware may find my efforts of some help in understanding how such awareness and knowledge are possible. At the very least it is to be hoped that some for whom religious knowledge is decidedly not an actuality will come to see how it is at least a possibility for others.

I gratefully acknowledge the assistance of the Southwestern at Memphis Committee on Research and Creative Activity, whose grant made it possible for me to spend a whole summer working on this book. In addition many of my teachers and students have both contributed to and put up with the development of the ideas expressed in this book. I thank them for their insights and patience. Finally, I am grateful to Professor Arthur Holmes who made a number of valuable suggestions at key points.

J.H.G.

Table of Contents

Part One

THE PROBLEM:
THE FATE OF MODERN PHILOSOPHY

I: The Contemporary Stalemate: Epistemological Dualism

Contemporary philosophy and theology are both characterized by a good deal of antipathy between the movements known as existentialism and positivism. Although there are some prospects that this antipathy can be at least partially overcome by a rapprochement between the offspring of these two movements, namely, phenomenology and linguistic analysis, Western culture is still largely dominated by the conflict between them. It is not my purpose to deny the reality of this conflict. What I would like to do is suggest that this antipathy is actually symptomatic of a much more profound *agreement* between the two movements. In short, both existentialism and positivism rest upon a common foundation that is the real source of much of the philosophical and theological tension of our day.

Perhaps the best way to zero in on this common foundation is in terms of the distinction commonly held to exist between "fact" and "value." Indeed, it is the very commonplaceness of this distinction that makes it so insidious! Everyone in our age is certain that facts and values are entirely distinct and unrelated to one another, and that therefore the scientific and humanistic disciplines are also unrelated to one another. This is an "established fact" of our day. In other words, what existentialism and positivism have in common is the agreement (nonetheless real for often being tacit) that there is an unbridgeable gulf between the domains of fact and value. But though they agree on this dichotomy between mankind's major concerns, the two movements disagree about which of the two concerns is more important. It is the agreement concerning the dichotomy on which I want to focus in this chapter. Dealing first with philosophy, I want to document the claim that positivism is founded upon this dichotomy between fact and value. (Anyone at all familiar with A. J. Ayer's *Language, Truth and Logic* and like-minded works in the social sciences will be aware that the claim hardly needs substantiation.) Next, I will attempt to substantiate the claim that existentialism is founded upon the same basic dichotomy. To oversimplify: While positivism maintains the ultimacy of fact and belittles value as emotive, existentialism maintains the ultimacy of value and demeans factuality as shallow. The final part of the chapter will trace the same foundational dichotomy in the "positivist" and existentialist movements of theology. My thesis is that this all-pervasive dichotomy has led to a stalemate, the outcome of which is intellectual schizophrenia, both culturally and individually.

It should be noted at the outset that there are serious limitations inherent in using any terms for designating such a pervasive cultural phenomenon as the dichotomy under consideration. I have chosen "fact" and "value" as the chief labels for the two sides of the dichotomy, hoping to fill out the meaning of these terms by using other terms that have the same basic function in various other contexts. It might be argued that the label "fact-meaning dichotomy" would serve better, since "meaning" is a broader term than "value." But in the sense that both "value" and "meaning" can be used to mean "significance," I would view them as synonymous. What I wish to contend, then, is that in our day "factuality" (what *is* the case) and "significance" (what the facts *mean*) are viewed as totally distinct. Thus throughout the discussion the terms "fact" and "value" are deliberately used in a broad sense so as to bring together a variety of, but basically similar, emphases.

1. FACT AND VALUE IN PHILOSOPHY

Speaking of the rift that characterizes contemporary philosophy, Walter Kaufmann makes the following comment:

> It is one of the saddest features of our age that we are faced with an entirely unnecessary dichotomy: on the one hand there are those whose devotion to intellectual cleanliness and rigor is exemplary but who refuse to deal with anything but small, and often downright trivial, questions; in the other camp are men like Toynbee and some of the existentialists who deal with the big and interesting questions, but in such a manner that the positivists point to them as living proofs that any effort of this kind is doomed to failure. Aware of their opponents' errors, both sides go to ever greater extremes; the split widens; and the intelligent layman who is left in the middle will soon lose sight of both.[1]

The contention of this chapter is that the basic reason for this widening gap between the two main motifs of philosophy is their mutual acceptance of an absolute distinction between judgments of fact and judgments of value. At one extreme stands logical empiricism and at the other stands existentialism; and yet in the matter of accepting the fact-value dichotomy the extremes meet.

Although there is a good deal of diversity among the various philosophers generally classified as logical empiricists, there is also a great deal of unanimity with respect to the point under consideration. I should like to document this unanimity in the writings of three of the more influential members of this school of thought—the early Ludwig Wittgenstein, Hans Reichenbach, and Paul Edwards.

After writing his first major work, the *Tractatus Logico-Philosophicus,* Wittgenstein withdrew from philosophy convinced that he had solved its major problems and disillusioned by how unimportant these solutions seemed. More than ten years later he returned to philosophy because he became convinced that there was still work to be done. In 1929, the first year of his return, he gave a lecture on ethics. Although there seems to be little difference between the *Tractatus* and this lecture with respect to the relation between the domains of fact and value, Wittgenstein's insistence upon the dichotomy between the two comes out more clearly in the lecture.

Wittgenstein begins his lecture by making a distinction between the "relative" and "absolute" uses of the term "good," stating that the relative use is always made in relation to some chosen end and that it can thus be rephrased in a way that is free from ethical implications. He then goes on to state the main thesis of the lecture: "Now what I wish to contend is that, although all judgments of relative value can be shown to be mere statements of facts, no statement of fact can ever be, or imply, a judgment of absolute value."[2] Clearly, he intends "absolute" to be synonymous with "ethical."

A bit later in the lecture Wittgenstein equates "meaningfulness" with judgments of fact and concludes that judgments of value are devoid of cognitive meaning.[3] He then maintains that

> ...in ethical and religious language we seem constantly to be using similes. But a simile must be the simile for *something*. And if I can describe a fact by means of a simile I must also be able to drop the simile and to describe the facts without it. Now in our case [that of value judgments] as soon as we try to drop the simile and simply to state the facts which stand behind it, we find that there are no such facts.[4]

The positivist overtones of these statements are obvious. The world of discourse has been divided into two entirely separate domains, and cognitive significance has been reserved for the factual domain. In this lecture Wittgenstein also states that the domains of experience that lie "behind" those of language are likewise entirely separate.[5]

In his book *The Rise of Scientific Philosophy,* Hans Reichenbach traces the revolt of logical empiricism against the more traditional rationalism of both ancient and modern philosophy and makes the standard distinction between logical and empirical knowledge, the former being defined in terms of tautologies (analytic propositions) and the latter in terms of probabilities (synthetic propositions). Upon this foundational interpretation of the nature of cognitive knowledge Reichenbach proceeds to build his understanding of ethics. His central theme is this: "The modern analysis of knowledge makes a cognitive ethics impossible: knowledge does not include any normative parts and therefore does not lend itself to an interpretation of ethics."[6] Here he follows David Hume in maintaining that "is-statements" and "ought-statements" have nothing in common, in the sense that the one cannot be derived from the other.

Reichenbach, like many empiricist philosophers, interprets ethical statements, indeed all value judgments, as directives or imperatives, which are to be clearly distinguished from assertions. The latter are subject to true and false judgments, while the former are subject only to being obeyed or disobeyed. Thus these two sets of statements have distinct kinds of meaning:

> Although imperatives are neither true nor false, they are understood by other persons and therefore have a meaning, which may be called an *instrumental meaning*. It is to be distinguished from the *cognitive meaning* of statements, defined in the verifiability theory of meaning.[7]

Reichenbach goes on to defend this interpretation of ethical discourse as both functional and devoid of immoralist implications, but the fact remains that his interpretation reflects an absolute dichotomy between the realms of fact and value.

That such expressions of the positivist dichotomy between fact and value are not passé is illustrated in a recent article by Paul Edwards. Writing on "Professor Tillich's Confusions," Edwards mounts a thorough and interesting case against the philosophical theology of Paul Tillich, arguing that according to any understanding of his terms, Tillich's statements about God are "meaningless" or "unintelligible."[8] In making his case, Edwards aligns himself with "reconstructed positivism" by accepting the premise that metaphorical sentences often possess certain features that make them meaningless.

Edwards zeros in on Tillich's use of metaphorical and analogical language in an attempt to speak about God. While granting all along that such language may well have an emotional or valuational function, Edwards maintains that it does not have any cognitive or factual function. The metaphorical use of language can be said to have cognitive meaning only when it is "reducible" to non-metaphorical, or factual, language. Edwards says:

> In these cases we know perfectly well what the authors mean although they are using certain words metaphorically. But we know this because we can eliminate the metaphorical expression, because we can specify the content of the assertion in non-metaphorical language, because we can supply the literal equivalent. . . . In calling a metaphor "reducible" all I mean is that the truth-claims made by the sentence in which it occurs can be reproduced by one or more sentences all of whose components are used in literal senses. . . . When a sentence contains an irreducible metaphor, it follows at once that the sentence is devoid of cognitive meaning, that it is unintelligible, that it fails to make a genuine assertion.[9]

By thus arguing against the possibility of irreducible metaphorical language being cognitively meaningful, Edwards ultimately relies upon the major premise of logical empiricism, namely that knowledge is limited to the language of logic and science. Thus once again the dichotomy between factual judgments and value judgments makes its appearance. Statements are classified according to two broad categories: those yielding knowledge because they can be judged true or false, tautological or contradictory; and those accomplishing other tasks such as expressing emotions and making value judgments. Any attempt to synthesize or relate these two kinds of statements results in unintelligibility.

Let us turn now to the other major philosophical movement on the contemporary scene, existentialism. The existentialists are diametrically opposed to the positivist emphasis on the area of fact, emphasizing instead the area of value. Yet they share with the logical empiricists a conviction that the two areas have little, if anything, in common.

One of the more influential exponents of existentialist philosophy is Martin Heidegger, and an examination of his thought—difficult as it is—will reveal his dependence upon a basic split between the world of fact and the world of value. This dependence can be seen most clearly in his understanding of the nature of language and the task of philosophy. It has proved helpful in recent years to distinguish the "early Heidegger" from the "later Heidegger," and the following sketch of his thought will make use of this distinction.[10]

The view of language in the work of the early Heidegger is difficult to classify. On the one hand, Heidegger was aware of the serious shortcomings of the logically objective language employed by philosophers throughout the ages. Although the Greek philosophers of the middle classical period—such as Socrates and Plato—used a more flexible and experiential language, the dominant model for language from Aristotle down to modern times has been logic. And as a result of the dominance of logic and of the rise of scientific discourse, language since the time of Descartes has increasingly been used in a way that necessitates a dichotomy between subject and object. Heidegger saw both of these factors as destructive to an adequate view of reality because they emphasize the importance of what lies outside of the subject, to the exclusion of what lies within him. Since, on Heidegger's view, the particulars of the individual subject's experience are the most real, it is the objective use of language that actually results in the most "subjective" view of life, in the sense that it fails to take into account that which is most real. Such objectivity has permeated traditional metaphysics. For this reason, the early Heidegger sought to "overcome metaphysics" by overcoming the tyranny of objectivity in which it had become imprisoned. The subject, and not the object, became the primary focus in Heidegger's early thought.

On the other hand, even a cursory reading of *Being and Time* is sufficient to establish the fact that for all his concern with overcoming the tyranny of objectivity, Heidegger made almost exclusive use of technical and abstract language. Indeed, his early writing was as much in the tradition of Hegel as it was in that of Kierkegaard or any other existentialist! It appears that Heidegger sought to correct the mistakes of traditional metaphysics by changing its focus and subject matter, but not by changing its conceptual and analytical tools. Although there seem to be intimations in the early writings of the change that was to take place in his thought, especially in the concepts of primordial discourse, listening and silence, Heidegger was essentially attempting to undermine traditional metaphysics by means of its own conceptual tools and rules. Like Sartre, who in some ways is involved in the same difficulty, the early Heidegger, a so-called existential-phenomenologist, is open to the charge of actually being a rationalist. It was in realizing this discrepancy in his early thought that Heidegger changed his approach.

This turn is exhibited in the lecture on "Hölderlin and the Essence of Poetry" given in 1937,[11] and its results can be seen in "The Way Back Into the Ground of Metaphysics" of 1949.[12] These two brief essays are mentioned here not only because they are clear and representative, but also because they are among the few pieces of writing to come from Heidegger's pen in recent years.

The major shift in Heidegger's thought pertains to the nature of philosophical thought and language. As I have indicated, Heidegger's efforts to overcome traditional metaphysics by means of the traditional tools of objective thought and language were doomed from the start. The methodology appropriate to a proper response to true being is one which, instead of attempting to objectify being, allows being to speak through the response. For this reason, Heidegger now maintains that poetic thought and speech are most appropriate to the task of the philosopher. The poet "understands" being in such a way as not to force it into conceptual and linguistic molds, but rather to become a channel through which being can reveal itself. Thus the philosopher should approach being in attentive silence, and think and speak in the manner of the poet, not in the manner of the logician.

It is plain that this new direction in Heidegger's thinking bears as strong a resemblance to mysticism as it does to existentialism. The whole attempt to conceptualize and analyze the phenomena of existential experience has been set aside as unfortunate in both content and method. At times, Heidegger seems to maintain that this whole revolution was incipient within his early approach and could not have been accomplished apart from it. Only by attempting to dismantle traditional metaphysics by means of its own tools could one come to see the need for an entirely new approach. At any rate, the new approach has taken shape, and the philosopher is now encouraged to learn from the poet.

> It is in the poetic mode that language is born. . . . Hence poetry never takes language as a raw material ready to hand, rather it is poetry which first makes language possible. Poetry is the primitive language of a historical people.[13]

The view of language implied by this new approach is best set forth by Heidegger himself in the paper he wrote for the Second Drew University Consultation on Hermeneutics in April of 1964.[14] Heidegger addressed himself to the theme of this conference, namely, "The Problem of Non-objectifying Thinking and Speaking." Heidegger proposes to get at the nature and possibility of non-objectifying thought and speech by means of closely related questions about the meaning of the terms "objectifying," "thinking," and "speaking," and whether or not all thought and speech are objectifying. Before taking up these questions, he makes three introductory remarks that provide a context for his subsequent discussion. First, he notes the two extreme, diametrically opposed, views of language on the contemporary scene—Carnap's positivism and his own "poetism." The former views language as an objective, technical-logical system created and controlled by man. The latter views language as a speculative venture of response and submission which expresses the true nature of experience, and through which *being* speaks. Second, Bergson and Nietzsche to the contrary notwithstanding, Heidegger insists that not all language and thought are objectifying in nature. Although one cannot apply objectifying thought and speech to that area of experience to which it is not appropriate, the alternatives are not exhausted by silence (mysticism) and vitalist philosophers (Bergson and Nietzsche). The most appropriate alternative is that of non-objectifying thinking and speaking. Third, Heidegger points out that the suggestions which follow in his discussion are to be understood as questions, and not as answers, because of the mysterious nature of language. Language is primal and must be contemplated, not dogmatized about.

Heidegger defines "to objectify" as to make "something into an object." In spite of the confusion surrounding the history of subject-object epistemology from the Middle Ages through Descartes to Kant, it is still possible to reflect upon and speak about aspects of experience and reality without making them into objects. In Heidegger's own, rather cryptic words:

> When I am now given over in my silent speaking to the radiant red of the rose, and meditate on the redness of the rose, this redness is then neither an Object, nor a thing, nor a *Gegenstand* like the blooming rose. The rose stands in the garden, perhaps swaying to and fro in the breeze. The redness of the rose, on the other hand, neither stands in the garden nor can it sway to and fro in the breeze. Nevertheless I think it and speak of it in that I name it. Accordingly, there is a thinking and saying which in no way objectifies nor reifies.[15]

For Heidegger, "thinking" is defined in two ways. There is representational and assertive thinking and there is "the comportment permitting that which shows itself and how it shows itself to give to it what it has to say of that which appears." In other words, there is a form of thinking which overcomes the subject-object dichotomy of representational thinking and allows the mind to experience *being* directly. This is reminiscent of Kant's desire to overcome some of the limitations of speculative reason by means of practical reason, although Heidegger is more mystically inclined than was Kant.

Speaking, according to Heidegger, need not consist of representational symbols that can be analyzed objectively. "Is speaking in its own-most being not a saying, a manifold showing of that which hearing, i.e., the obedient attention to that which appears, lets be said?" He suggests that comforting a sick person with a kind word is an example of speaking without "manipulating objects."

On the basis of the foregoing definitions, Heidegger maintains that "every thinking is a speaking and every speaking a thinking." The traditional view of language has perpetuated a distinction between thought and speaking that does not correspond to experience. But since thinking is "a letting-be-said of that which shows itself," thinking and saying are actually united.

Heidegger concludes his consideration of the nature of non-objectifying thought and speech by asserting that although objectification has its place in scientific-technological enterprises, it is decidedly out of place in the endeavor to interpret *being*. Here the thinker must open himself to that which reveals itself in *being*. Only in this way can the tyranny of objectifying thought and speech that dominates contemporary culture be overthrown. Heidegger insists that the truth of these general theses needs no objective substantiation. "The very being of thinking and saying can only be apprehended in an unbiased sighting of the phenomena."[16]

In spite of the many vagaries and innuendoes in Heidegger's thought, this summary should make it quite clear that Heidegger operates on the basis of the dichotomy discussed throughout the first part of this chapter. The area of experience pertaining to value judgments must never be confused with the area pertaining to factual (objective) judgments. Moreover, according to Heidegger, the type of language that is appropriate to the latter is hopelessly inappropriate to the former. It is interesting to note the strong similarity in both tone and content existing between the positions of the early Wittgenstein and the later Heidegger with respect to the relation between the language of fact and value.

Another thinker who clearly expresses an existentialist point of view is José Ortega y Gasset. Like many other existentialists, Ortega takes as his starting point man's unique capacity for self-transcendence:

> ...man can, from time to time, suspend his direct concern with things, detach himself from his surroundings, ignore them, and subjecting his faculty of attention to a radical shift—incomprehensible zoologically—turn, so to speak, his back on the world and take his stand inside himself, attend to his own inwardness or, what is the same thing, concern himself with himself and not with what is *other*, with things.[17]

This quotation pinpoints Ortega's basic dualism with respect to human existence. Man has both an "outside" realm and an "inside" realm. It is not long before this dualism gives way to a rather extensive argument against the overemphasis in our age of the external, or behavioral, realm of human existence. Finally, this line of argument leads to a position that implies that the whole of the external, objective world of human existence is not really important.

What is of ultimate importance, especially for philosophy, according to Ortega, is that side of human life which deals with value judgments. The positivist attempt to view philosophy as a science is dismissed by Ortega as a "brief attack of modesty" in which philosophers sought to abdicate their true responsibility.

> Philosophy, then, is the criticism of conventional life—including, and most particularly, of his own life—which man finds himself needing to undertake from time to time, haling his conventional life before the judgment-seat of his genuine life, of his inexorable solitude.[18]

Thus we find again the assumption that human experience is to be divided into two totally distinct areas. Empiricists emphasize the factual, while existentialists emphasize the valuational. Both insist that the two are essentially different.

In his now famous example of the student who could not decide whether to stay with his mother or to go fight with the resistance movement, Jean-Paul Sartre maintains that in the last analysis it is action ("deeds") that decides moral issues, and not feelings or reasonings:

> In other words, feeling is formed by the deeds that one does; therefore I cannot consult it as a guide to action. And that is to say that I can neither seek within myself for an authentic impulse to action, nor can I expect, from some ethic, formulae that will enable me to act. You may say that the youth did, at least, go to a professor to ask for advice. But if you seek counsel—from a priest, for example—you have selected that priest; and at bottom you already know, more or less, what he would advise. In other words, to choose an adviser is nevertheless to commit oneself by that choice. If you are a Christian, you will say, Consult a priest; but there are collaborationists, priests who are resisters and priests who wait for the tide to turn: which will you choose? Had this young man chosen a priest of the resistance, or one of the collaboration, he would have decided beforehand the kind of advice he was to receive. Similarly, in coming to me, he knew what advice I should give him, and I had but one reply to make. You are free, therefore choose—that is to say, invent.[19]

This "action-centered" variety of existentialism expressed so forcefully by Sartre also segregates the rational or objective side of human experience from its volitional or subjective side. In arguing for the priority of the volitional side as opposed to the rational side, Sartre is implicitly arguing for the complete autonomy of the two sides. Here again the fact-value dualism reveals itself. For although Sartre would seem to have a trichotomy rather than a dichotomy, it remains true that for him value, or meaning, lies on the side of volition and not on the side of reason or facts.

2. FACT AND VALUE IN THEOLOGY

Whether theology is dependent on philosophy for its direction is an interesting question. Be that as it may, it is an incontestable fact that contemporary theology is characterized largely by the same dualistic tension that has characterized contemporary philosophy. There is a theological "positivism" which stresses an objectivist, or cognitive, interpretation of religion; and there is a theological "existentialism" which stresses a subjectivist, or valuational interpretation of religion. Although the lines between these two emphases are not as clearly drawn in theology as they are in philosophy, there is sufficient tension between the two to point up the common assumption that there are essentially two ways of viewing religion.

By way of clarification, it should be mentioned that another point upon which logical empiricism and existentialism agree is their mutual dissatisfaction with all forms of rationalism. The attempt to come to an understanding of reality by means of a systematic, rational process—as exemplified by Descartes—is rejected by both schools of contemporary philosophy. Similarly, the opposing sides of contemporary theology agree that traditional theology, which often sought to base the claims of Christianity upon a rational appeal to deductive arguments and miraculous events, is to be rejected. Nevertheless, as is the case with philosophy, the theological scene is still characterized by a fundamental tension that calls attention to a dichotomy between the realms of cognitivity and non-cognitivity.

On the one side of today's theological scene stands what is usually termed "neo-orthodox" theology, and on the other side stands "existentialist" theology. Though both have roots in the thought of Søren Kierkegaard, the former emphasizes a doctrinal and conceptual interpretation of Christianity, while the latter focuses on an ethical and volitional interpretation. But behind this contrast of emphases stands a mutually held assumption that these two aspects of religious experience are essentially different. In what follows I will analyze representative thinkers on both sides of this debate with an eye to pointing up their common dependence upon this foundational assumption. Since both the major movements in contemporary theology draw heavily upon Kierkegaard's thought, it would seem advisable to begin with a rather thorough analysis of his position on the relation between objectivity and subjectivity in religion.[20] I will move then to a briefer consideration of the thought of Karl Barth and William Hordern, as representatives of neo-orthodoxy, and that of Rudolph Bultmann and Paul Tillich as representatives of existentialist theology.

Kierkegaard inherited his philosophical problems from Hegel. Hegel's "Absolute Idealism" unites the nature and structure of the mind (Idealism) with the nature and structure of transcendent reality (the Absolute). The originality, profundity, and comprehensiveness of Hegel's philosophy made it the most influential ideology of the nineteenth century. It even effected a marriage between philosophy and Christian theology.

In his *Philosophical Fragments,* Kierkegaard analyzes the epistemology of idealism, contrasting it to that of New Testament Christianity. He concludes that the marriage between the two is a mistake and must be annulled. It is my contention that in his attempt to overcome Hegel's identification of idealistic philosophy with Christian theology, Kierkegaard espoused an absolute dichotomy between knowledge and faith. I offer this quotation from his Journal as an initial substantiation of my claim:

> But such a scientific method becomes especially dangerous and pernicious when it would encroach also upon the sphere of spirit. Let it deal with plants and animals and stars in that way; but to deal with the human spirit in that way is blasphemy, which only weakens ethical and religious passion. Even the act of eating is more reasonable than speculating with a microscope upon the functions of digestion....A dreadful sophistry spreads microscopically and telescopically into tomes, and yet in the last resort produces nothing, qualitatively understood, though it does, to be sure, cheat men out of the simple,

profound and passionate wonder which gives impetus to the
ethical....The only thing certain is the ethical-religious.[21]

In the first chapter of *Philosophical Fragments* Kierkegaard sets forth the idealist epistemology and contrasts it to
that of New Testament Christianity. Classical idealism
maintains that knowledge is obtained by rational, introspective dialectic. Plato's doctrine of "recollection,"
Descartes' concept of "intuition," and Hegel's doctrine of
"the truth as the whole" all exemplify this approach. The
presupposition that underlies such doctrines is that knowledge is a matter of the learner's becoming aware of what is
already within him. In other words, there is an essential
unity between the knower and ultimate reality, which
enables the mind of the knower to reflect reality—even
though this unity is very often hidden behind the vicissi-
tudes of sensory experience.

The logical corollary of this position is that time,
history, and individual existence must be viewed as non-
essential and irrelevant to truth and knowledge. All such
factors become mere accidental "occasions" for the re-
flecting of eternal truth. To put it differently, the original
relationship between the mind and reality is one of harmony and continuity, with particulars serving simply to
disclose this unity to the knower.

Over against this view Kierkegaard sets an alternative
view which maintains that time, history, and individual
existence are essential in coming to know truth. Although
he introduces this view as a tentative "thought project,"
Kierkegaard takes this to be the epistemological position
of New Testament Christianity. The underlying presupposition of this approach is that knowledge is a unique
achievement that actually effects something in the learner
which was not there before. The particular temporal experiences of the existing individual thus become extremely
important as decisive media of knowledge.[22] In this position the original relation between the mind and reality is
one of discontinuity, with particulars serving to bridge the
gap between the two.

Kierkegaard spends a good deal of time in the latter part of Chapter One and in Chapter Two developing some of the theological implications of this epistemological picture. He maintains that in the view which places real value on the particulars of time and individuality, not only is the learner originally without knowledge, he is without the basic condition or ability to receive knowledge as well. Thus, unless someone (God Himself) supplies him with the condition (faith) whereby he can receive the truth, the learner will always remain without knowledge. To put it philosophically, the ego-centric predicament will consign the learner to skepticism. Moreover, the teacher (God) must provide this condition by descending to the level of the learner, and not by insisting that the learner ascend to the level of the teacher. All of this renders the specific relationship between the learner and the teacher ("the Moment," when knowledge is obtained) extremely significant and decisive.

The idea that the mind of the knowing subject can ever transcend the ego-centric predicament, and move from ignorance of reality to knowledge of it, is a paradox, which cannot be grasped by reason. Put theologically, the paradox is that God (as teacher) would descend to the level of the learner in order to provide him with the faith which enables him to know the truth. Either man has knowledge or he does not. If he has it, as in classical idealism, then all he needs is reminding. If he does not have it, as New Testament Christianity holds, then it would seem illogical to conceive of his ever obtaining it because he would not recognize it when confronted with it. And yet, Christianity holds that knowledge can be obtained. This is the "Absolute Paradox" delineated in Chapter Three of the *Fragments* and summarized in Chapter Four:

> Unless the God grants the condition which makes it possible to understand this, how is it to be supposed that the learner will be able to discover it! But that the God himself gives this condition has been shown above to be a consequence of the *Moment,* and it has also been shown that the Moment is the

> Paradox, and that without it we are unable to advance, but
> return to Socrates.[23]

Kierkegaard maintains that reason must reject such a paradox as meaningless, for it is unable to grasp something that thought cannot think. Although many efforts have been made to distinguish between paradox and contradiction in order to protect Kierkegaard from being labeled an irrationalist, the opening pages of Chapter Three of the *Fragments* make it clear that Kierkegaard uses "paradox" as a synonym for "rational contradiction." One simply cannot, according to Kierkegaard, expect pure, speculative reason to perform beyond its inherent limitations. By means of human reason there is no way to obtain knowledge of reality, nor to break out of the limitations of the ego-centric predicament. The attempt to apply reason to ultimate reality only ends in contradiction.[24] Furthermore, Kierkegaard devotes a good deal of space to criticizing the traditional proofs of God's existence. He argues that deductive proofs are circular and irrelevant to questions of existence, while inductive arguments do not yield proof because the evidence is never all in. Thus he concludes that a strict, rational knowledge of reality, including God, is absolutely impossible.

In the Appendix to Chapter Three, Kierkegaard asserts that the only way out of this skeptical situation (the way made possible by Christianity) is for reason to admit its limitations and set itself aside in order to make room for faith. Only an active, passionate faith can embrace and accept the paradox. This does not mean that the learner "understands" the paradox, but only that he, by reason, understands that it is a paradox, and accepts it as such by faith. Thus, it is only by means of a "leap" that the knower is able to transcend the ego-centric predicament. He cannot know *how* he has obtained knowledge, but he can know *that* he has obtained it. He cannot understand it, but he can experience it.

> We do not ask that he understand the Paradox but only
> understand that this is the Paradox. How this takes place we

have already shown. It comes to pass when the Reason and the Paradox encounter one another happily in the Moment, when the Reason sets itself aside and the Paradox bestows itself. The third entity in which this union is realized (for it is not realized in the Reason, since it is set aside: nor in the Paradox, which bestows itself—hence it is realized *in* something) is that happy passion to which we will now assign a name, though it is not the name that so much matters. We shall call this passion: *Faith*. [25]

In Chapters Four and Five, and in the interlude between them, Kierkegaard raises the question of the nature of religious faith. In the case of the disciple who was contemporaneous with the historical Christ (Chapter Four), it is clear that faith was not dependent upon a knowledge of the historical circumstances concerning Jesus. Nor was it dependent upon the disciple's knowledge of Jesus' teachings. Both of these served only as "occasions for self-understanding." It would seem that for Kierkegaard faith is not a form of knowledge at all, since "no knowledge can have for its object the absurdity that the Eternal is the historical."[26] In like fashion, faith is not an act of the will, since such an act presupposes the ability to grasp the truth—and man does not have this ability. In fact, faith itself is this ability (or condition) to grasp the truth, and it must be given by God.

Faith, then, is neither knowledge nor act, but a miraculous gift of God enabling the disciple to accept the paradox that "knowledge" of God (reality) is possible. I have put quotation marks around the term "knowledge" because Kierkegaard uses it in an ambiguous manner. On the one hand, he appears to maintain that cognitive (propositional) knowledge of God is impossible, and on the other hand, he seems to maintain that experiential knowledge of God is possible. I cannot discuss this point further here. Suffice it to say that Kierkegaard is not sufficiently clear in his use of the term "knowledge." But it is clear that he wants an "absolute, qualitative distinction" drawn between "knowledge" in the scientific or philosophic sense and "faith" in the religious sense.

What holds for those disciples who were contemporaneous with the historical Jesus also holds for those who are not contemporaneous. If faith were dependent upon knowing the historical facts, all "second-hand" disciples down through the ages would be at a decided disadvantage—and, indeed, could not be said to have faith at all. Thus it is that religious faith must be defined as completely independent of all forms of human knowledge. That God revealed himself in history can be received by faith alone.

> The historical fact for a contemporary is that the God has *come into existence;* for the member of a later generation the historical fact is that the God has been present through *having come into existence.* Herein precisely lies the contradiction. No one can become immediately contemporary with this historical fact, as has been shown in the preceding; it is the object of Faith, since it concerns coming into existence. No question is here raised as to the true content of this; the question is if one will give assent to the God's having come into existence, by which the God's eternal essence is inflected in the dialectical determination of coming into existence.[27]

In the final pages of the *Fragments,* Kierkegaard sets forth one of the most important implications of this account of faith. It must be noted, in passing, that there is a definite sense in which this implication undercuts Kierkegaard's original distinction between classical idealism, in which the particular is irrelevant, and New Testament Christianity in which the particular is of decisive importance. Kierkegaard reasons that since faith is independent of any and all forms of knowledge about the historical Jesus, such knowledge serves only as an "occasion" (his term!) for confronting the individual with the paradoxical claim that God has made himself knowable to mankind. In the same way, the testimony of other believers serves only as a pointer to the ultimate reality which is to be accepted by faith. For this reason the reliability of the particular witness is essentially unimportant. The following quotation clearly states Kierkegaard's rather perplexing point:

If the fact spoken of were a simple historical fact, the accuracy of the historical sources would be of great importance. Here this is not the case, for Faith cannot be distilled from even the nicest accuracy of detail. The historical fact that the God has been in human form is the essence of the matter; the rest of the historical detail is not even as important as if we had to do with a human being instead of with the God. Jurists say that a capital crime submerges all lesser crimes, and so it is with Faith. Its absurdity makes all petty difficulties vanish. Inconsistencies which would otherwise be disconcerting do not count for anything here; they make no difference whatsoever. But it does make a difference on the contrary, if someone by petty calculation should try to auction off faith to the highest bidder; it makes so much difference as to prevent him from ever becoming a believer. If the contemporary generation had left nothing behind them but these words: "We have believed that in such and such a year the God appeared among us in the humble figure of a servant, that he lived and taught in our community, and finally died," it would be more than enough. The contemporary generation would have done all that was necessary; for this little advertisement, this *nota bene* on a page of universal history, would be sufficient to afford an occasion for a successor, and the most voluminous account can in all eternity do nothing more.[28]

Having laid out the philosophical skeleton of his position in the *Fragments*, Kierkegaard proceeded to "clothe" it with religious significance in the *Concluding Unscientific Postscript*. This work delineates the dichotomy between objective knowledge and subjective faith even more forcefully than does the *Fragments*. In fact, the *Postscript* is divided into two books, the first of which is concerned with "the objective problem concerning the truth of Christianity," and the second of which is concerned with "the subjective problem concerning the truth of Christianity." Only the first book and the first part of the second book are integral to our present considerations.

After stating the problem in terms of the possibility of basing one's eternal happiness upon a particular historical fact, Kierkegaard proceeds to examine the relevance of historical knowledge to Christian faith. Although the attempt to establish the truth of Christianity on objective historical facts takes various forms—such as scriptural reliability, ecclesiastical authority, and longevity—the results are always negative. The reason for this is not that the objective truth of such arguments cannot be established, but rather that even if it could be established, this would not have the slightest effect upon the status of one's faith. Nor would the inability to establish such arguments have any effect on faith. In fact, such concern with objective proof is a clear indication of the loss of faith!

> Here is the crux of the matter, and I come back to the case of the learned theology. For whose sake is it that the proof is sought? Faith does not need it; aye, it must even regard the proof as its enemy. But when faith begins to feel embarrassed and ashamed, like a young woman for whom her love is no longer sufficient, but who secretly feels ashamed of her lover and must therefore have it established that there is something remarkable about him—when faith thus begins to lose its passion, when faith begins to cease to be faith, then a proof becomes necessary so as to command respect from the side of unbelief. And as for the rhetorical stupidities that have been perpetrated by clergymen in connection with this matter, through a confusion of the categories—alas, let us not speak of them.[29]

Next, Kierkegaard briefly examines the relevance of objective, speculative reason to Christian faith. Here, too, the conclusion is negative. Philosophical speculation is fine in its place, but one must never allow it to be confused with religious faith.

> Christianity does not lend itself to objective observation, precisely because it proposes to intensify subjectivity to the utmost; and when the subject has thus put himself in the right attitude, he cannot attach his eternal happiness to speculative philosophy.[30]

In the first part of Book Two, Kierkegaard discusses the relation between knowledge and faith in connection with the philosophy of Lessing. First, Lessing was supposed to have maintained (and Kierkegaard expresses some doubt about his actual beliefs) that since there is an absolute distinction between eternal truth and factual knowledge, the former could never be dependent upon the latter. The eternal truth can be known only by a "leap" out of the realm of factual knowledge. Now although Kierkegaard thinks that Lessing confuses the issue of contemporaneity, he admires him for having seen the basic disjunction between these two realms:

> I refer to the fact that he religiously shut himself up within the isolation of his own subjectivity; that he did not permit himself to be deceived into becoming world-historic and systematic with respect to the religious, but understood and knew how to hold fast to the understanding that the religious concerned Lessing, and Lessing alone, just as it concerns every other human being in the same manner, understood that he had infinitely to do with God, and nothing, nothing to do with any man directly.[31]

Second, Lessing also said that "if God held all truth in His right hand, and in His left hand held the lifelong pursuit of it, he would choose the left hand." Kierkegaard takes this to be a distinction between the way of speculative, religious knowledge and the way of existential, religious faith. He enters into a lengthy polemic against the concern for a Christian "system" of thought. In addition, Kierkegaard uses this distinction as the springboard for his detailed explanation of the nature and quality of the subjective mode of existence which he presents in the remainder of the *Postscript*. Indeed, Lessing's distinction could be said to be the banner under which Kierkegaard's "knight of faith" does battle!

> The existing individual who concentrates all his attention upon the circumstance that he is an existing individual, will welcome those words of Lessing about a persistent striving, as a beautiful saying. To be sure, it did not indeed win for its author an immortal fame, because it is very simple; but every thoughtful individual must needs confirm its truth.[32]

By way of summary, it may be said that Kierkegaard distinguishes between reason and faith not in order to call attention to two forms of knowledge, but in order to set faith, as an experience and a commitment, over against all forms of knowledge. He is not opting for subjectivity in matters of modes of existence. Nevertheless, he clearly maintains that such existential subjectivity—adequacy of life—is in no way dependent upon epistemological considerations. In Kierkegaard's approach, the realms of knowledge and faith would seem to be entirely separated. Yet it is certainly possible to maintain that Kierkegaard does offer "subjective knowledge" as a substitute for objective knowledge in matters of religion. Indeed he is often interpreted this way, and there are a number of passages in which he seems to be doing precisely that. Now it is this difference of interpretation that has generated the tension between the neo-orthodox and existentialist theologians. Neo-orthodox thinkers, who stress the doctrinal and conceptual aspects of religious faith, interpret Kierkegaard as propounding a new view of the way in which revelation is known, that is, a new form of religious knowledge. Existentialist thinkers, on the other hand, who stress the volitional and ethical aspects of religious faith, interpret Kierkegaard as maintaining that there is no such thing as religious knowledge. Thus neo-orthodox theology focuses on the *content* of Kierkegaard's thought while existentialist theology focuses on its *style*.

The concern of neo-orthodox thinkers with the theological content of Christian revelation places them on the "positivist" side of the fact-value dichotomy. Before proceeding, however, we should dispose of two possible misunderstandings. First, the sort of positivism expressed in the writings of Karl Barth and his followers is not an attempt to reduce theology to empirical science. Such an attempt would be closer to fundamentalism than to neo-orthodoxy. Barthian positivism is characterized by a conceptual concern, which is not the same as an informational concern. The similarity it bears to philosophical positivism or logical empiricism is in its contention that if theological statements are to be of real value, they must be subject to being judged as true or false. Of course, for

Barth, there *are* theological truths, while for positivists there are not.

The second misunderstanding to avoid is the assumption that neo-orthodox theologians have no interest in the volitional or ethical side of Christian faith. By and large empiricist philosophers think that ethics is not of first-order philosophical significance. Barth and his followers, however, do think that Christian ethics is important, but only after full consideration has been given to theology. The similarity between this position and philosophical positivism is in the ancillary position each assigns to the valuational realm. Theological positivism is perhaps less exclusivist than its philosophical counterpart, but it is still based upon a strict line of demarcation between the cognitive (factual) and non-cognitive (valuational) realms of experience. Another way of viewing this similarity is to say that both philosophical and theological positivism maintain that ethical conclusions (ought) cannot be drawn from factual data (is).

There are two emphases in Barth's thought which point up the dichotomized nature of its foundation. The first is that there is such a thing as knowledge of God, and that its attainment is the goal of theology. Moreover, such knowledge is empirical in the sense that it is subject to confirmation.

> We are dealing with the possibility of knowing the Word of God. We are therefore dealing with the possibility of verifying the knowledge that men have of the Word of God. We are dealing with the fact that the Word of God may become true for men who became acquainted with it through revelation, Scripture, and proclamation, in such wise that they themselves must also hold it as true, that its trueness becomes their possession, that they become responsible witnesses of its truth. We are dealing with the fact that in truth the Church and Church proclamation, among men and through men, may take place in truth.[33]

This cognitive emphasis serves to differentiate Barth's thought from that of existentialist theologians such as Rudolph Bultmann who deny the possibility of a knowledge of God. For Barth one begins with the knowledge of God and theology, and then moves to ethics, which is seen as a matter of obeying a divine imperative. Although he does not draw the distinctions as precisely as do philosophers, Barth's contrast between knowing God and obeying God implies a split between the cognitive and non-cognitive realms that closely parallels that of logical empiricism.

The second emphasis in Barth's thought calling attention to his basic dualism is his insistence upon the absolute autonomy and uniqueness of the knowledge of God. In his view there is simply no way in which such knowledge can be obtained by even the qualified use of human cognitive capacities. When such knowledge is revealed it does not contradict these cognitive capacities, but it cannot be obtained through their use. Without entering into the theological questions that such a position raises, it can be seen readily that the exclusiveness of the position is similar to that exemplified by logical empiricism. Apart from revelation and faith, knowledge of God is totally impossible, no matter how wise the utterances of human wisdom might seem to be.

> ...it is with the real content of the real Word of God that man is likewise informed, that any power on his part to listen or understand or know, any capacity which he the creature, the sinner, the one who waits, might have to meet this Word with, and so any possibility in the first sense, does not enter into consideration, but that the possibility of knowing corresponding to the real Word of God has simply come to him, man, that it sets forth a quite inconceivable *novum* in direct contrast to all his ability and capacity, and is only to be regarded as a pure fact, like the Word of God itself.[34]

One of Barth's most articulate and influential followers is William Hordern. He too exemplifies the cognitive and autonomous emphases that reveal a basic dichotomy between the factual and valuational realms. Hordern's position, however, is less extreme than Barth's. Nonetheless, after he has qualified the concept of the knowledge of God by emphasizing that it is not to be equated with informational propositions about God, he still maintains that revelation provides a cognitive perspective from which one's understanding of reality is improved. With respect to the Word of God that is revealed in the Bible, Hordern argues that this view "emphasizes the objectivity of the revelation given by God and mediated to us through the Bible, and thus preserves the Reformers' emphasis upon the objectively given revelation in the Bible."[35]

On the matter of the absolute autonomy and uniqueness of the knowledge of God, Hordern is in essential agreement with Barth. He maintains that the criterion by means of which the knowledge claims of Christianity are to be judged cannot bear any relationship to the standard criteria used in other epistemological questions. For man to use ordinary rational and pragmatic criteria to judge the truth of God's revelation would be at best stupid and at worst blasphemous.[36]

> We have argued that in the nature of the case it would be irrational to expect to have criteria by which we could judge a revelation from God. The revelation must provide its own criteria of judgment. Christian faith is not a conclusion from a rational analysis of the universe but is a basic commitment of the self in response to the self-authenticating nature of the revelation claim. But we have tried to show that there is nothing irrational about this. On the contrary, with the coming of faith, reasoning does not end, but it begins, for it obtains a new perspective from which it can see reality.[37]

The point here, of course, is not to enter into the question of whether this is an adequate interpretation of the Christian position, but rather to make clear the fact that this interpretation implies as its basis a radical dichotomy between revelation and faith. They are not presented as being opposed, but they are presented as being essentially different in kind. Revelation is viewed as a cognitive perspective while faith is viewed as a volitional response. Such a distinction is essentially parallel to the fact-value distinction of contemporary empiricism.

Set over against neo-orthodox theology is Bultmannian theology, whose primal concern for the volitional and ethical interpretation of Christian revelation places it on the existentialist side of the fact-value dichotomy. The parallel between the positions of philosophical and theological existentialism is much more clear-cut than is the parallel between the corresponding forms of "positivism." Both Bultmann and Tillich interpret Kierkegaard to deny that there is such a thing as religious knowledge.

Bultmann's existentialist interpretation of Christian faith and theology is characterized by an unrelenting effort to eliminate any trace of cognitivity. For Bultmann there is no point to talking about a knowledge of God, nor about a conceptual understanding of revelation or theology. What there *is* a point to talking about is the existential nature of human life and the "posture of adequacy" with which the Christian gospel confronts mankind. The basic questions of human existence, such as meaningfulness, anxiety, and death, pertain to the attitudinal or volitional aspect of human experience. Thus Bultmann is strongly opposed to Barth's concern for the conceptual, or cognitive, interpretation of Christianity. The difference between the two thinkers' approaches is exhibited in the fact that Barth's major theological contribution is his multi-volume *Church Dogmatics,* while Bultmann's is an account of *The Theology of the New Testament.*

The heart of the existentialist attitudinal interpretation lies in a systematic effort to demythologize the New Testament in order to free the "life stance" of the gospel (the kerygma) from its conceptual wrappings of first-century mythology. Such a process clearly operates on the assumption that reality and human experience are divided into two realms, the factual, or cognitive, and the valuational, or non-cognitive. The Christian claim is said to have to do only with the latter, since it is concerned with the quality of human existence and not with knowledge about the world. As Bultmann says:

> The real purpose of myth is not to present an objective picture of the world as it is, but to express man's understanding of himself in the world in which he lives. Myth should be interpreted not cosmologically, but anthropologically, or better still, existentially. Myth speaks of the power or the powers which man supposes he experiences as the ground and limit of his world and of his own activity and suffering. He describes these powers in terms derived from the visible world, with its tangible objects and forces, and from human life, with its feelings, motives, and potentialities. . . . Hence the importance of the New Testament mythology lies not in its imagery but in the understanding of existence which it enshrines.[38]

The dualistic nature of Bultmann's thought is also reflected in his position on the "historical Jesus" question. On the basis of both his textual scholarship and his existentialist interpretative procedure, he concludes that the quest for the historical Jesus is hopeless. Bultmann goes beyond this, however, to maintain that the attempt to ground one's Christian faith in knowledge about Jesus' life and teachings is as un-Christian as it is hopeless. For Bultmann, there simply is no relation between the domains of fact and faith, and any attempt to ground the latter in the former is an expression of one's lack of faith.

> Like the doctrine of justification, de-mythologizing destroys every longing for security. There is no difference between security based on good works and security built on objectifying knowledge. The man who desires to believe in God must know that he has nothing at his own disposal on which to build this faith, that he is, so to speak, in a vacuum. He who abandons every form of security shall find the true security.[39]

The theological position of Paul Tillich is very similar to that of Bultmann. The primary differences between the two men are in emphasis and terminology. Tillich, unlike Bultmann, is as much influenced by German idealism as he is by existentialist philosophy. Also, Tillich's position is not informed by biblical studies, as is Bultmann's. Nevertheless, Tillich also understands Christianity as more a matter of volition and existential posture than a matter of conceptual knowledge. To be sure, he often talks as if there is a sense in which it is proper to speak of the conceptual dimension of Christianity as true, but almost invariably this claim is either lost in the shuffle of his symbolic idealism, or it is contradicted by another claim to the effect that all that matters is the quality of one's faith. This oscillation in his position makes it difficult to classify Tillich, but it is my contention that at least some of his crucial emphases display the dichotomy that has been the burden of this chapter.

Tillich defines faith as "ultimate concern." After making it quite clear that he regards faith as essentially distinct from a knowledge of scientific and historical facts, Tillich goes on to maintain that although philosophy and faith both have ultimate reality as their object, they differ in that philosophy seeks to grasp it objectively and conceptually while faith seeks to symbolize and become involved with it. Tillich concludes by addressing himself to the question of the truth of faith in these words: "From the subjective side one must say that faith is truth if it adequately expresses an ultimate concern," while from the objective side one must say that faith is true if it focuses on an "ultimate which is really ultimate."[40] Unfortunately he never manages to develop a criterion for determining which ultimates are "really ultimate," and thus his definition of true faith becomes circular. In other words, Tillich's interpretation of faith as ultimate concern places him solidly on the non-cognitive or valuational side of the fact-value dichotomy.

The same result is obtained when one examines Tillich's view of the nature of talk about God. Although he modified his view from time to time, it seems that his more sensible and final view is that "the statement that God is being-itself is a nonsymbolic statement. It does not point beyond itself. It means what it says directly and properly. However, after this has been said, nothing else can be said about God as God which is not symbolic."[41] It would seem that purely symbolic talk about God cannot, according to Tillich's system, be said to yield any sort of knowledge, while the statement "God is being-itself" could be said to yield some sort of knowledge. However, precisely what sort of claim is made by this statement—and how it would be confirmed or disconfirmed—Tillich does not say. Once again he seems to have implicitly placed himself in the existentialist camp, and thereby to have betrayed his dependence upon the dichotomy between the realms of cognitivity and non-cognitivity.

The aim of this chapter has been twofold. I have sought, first, to document the claim that both contemporary philosophy and theology are characterized by a stalemate between two equally important, but mutually exclusive, points of view: positivism and existentialism. The nature of this stalemate consists in the fact that each of these two points of view stresses one major aspect of human experience and reality to the exclusion of the other. The empiricist movement in philosophy and the "positivist" movement in theology both stress the priority of cognition over valuation. The existentialist movement in these two fields focuses on the priority of valuation over cognition.

The second, and more basic, part of my concern has been to substantiate the claim that this contemporary stalemate has resulted from the shared assumption that there is an unbridgeable gap between those aspects of experience and reality known as the cognitive and the valuational. Once this common assumption is granted, it is hardly surprising that the twentieth-century thinker finds himself forced to choose between these two emphases, even though he is somehow aware that both are important. Thus the intellectual schizophrenia of our day is based upon an epistemological dualism which provides the ground rules within which intellectual activity is carried on.

II: Retracing the Steps: Nineteenth-Century Alternatives

It might well be asked at this point how the epistemological dualism pinpointed in the first chapter came about. There is good evidence that to a large extent it was inherited from the nineteenth century. My aim in this chapter, then, is to trace the main philosophical and theological movements of that century and to show that they can profitably be understood as having arisen in response to the same dichotomy. I will focus on the positions of G. W. F. Hegel, Friedrich Schleiermacher, and Ludwig Feuerbach, but will take account of various other thinkers as well.

Two preliminary remarks before beginning. The primary concern of this book is to attempt an epistemological reconstruction that will provide a sound basis for the possibility of religious knowledge. Thus while the broader epistemological issues will be given fairly thorough treatment, the focus will be increasingly on the possibility and nature of the knowledge of God. For this reason the following examination of nineteenth-century thought will concentrate on the question of religious epistemology. In the terms of the first chapter, it is my thesis that the dichotomy between the factual and valuational realms places the question of the possibility of the knowledge of God in a most precarious, if not impossible, position. The schizophrenia which results from being forced to live in two unrelated realms simultaneously was as prevalent in the nineteenth century as it is today.

Secondly, the following analysis of nineteenth-century thinkers will be understood much more fully against the background of a brief hint about where the argument of Part One is headed. In the next chapter I am going to argue that the most explicit source of the fact-value dichotomy is in the philosophy of Immanuel Kant. Thus the various positions to be examined in this chapter are best understood as responses to the various dichotomies espoused by Kant. Essentially the Kantian position boils down to placing an absolute gulf between what Kant called the "phenomenal world" (corresponding to the cognitive realm) and the "noumenal world" (corresponding to the non-cognitive realm). This is an ontological dualism. Kant further maintained that the phenomenal world is known by means of the categories of the understanding, but that the noumenal world cannot be known, except perhaps by means of the postulates of "practical," or ethical, reason. This is an epistemological dualism. Kant's conclusion was that religious matters must be relegated to the ethical domain exclusively. It was in response to these distinctions that the positions discussed on the following pages arose. A more thorough presentation of Kant's position will be taken up in the next chapter.

1. HEGEL: THE WAY OF SPECULATION

It might appear from a cursory reading of his major works that Hegel never gave much thought to the critical philosophy of Immanuel Kant. But upon a closer reading it becomes apparent that Hegel's thought represents, in fact, an absolute rejection of Kant's critique of speculative reason and knowledge of the noumenal world. Whereas Kant constructed an impassable gulf between human knowledge and ultimate reality, Hegel began with the assumption of a perfect correspondence, indeed identity, between the two. For Hegel, knowledge about reality is obtained by the rigorous application of speculative reason.

The methodology of Hegel's thought is perhaps most clearly presented in his philosophy of history. After distinguishing his approach to history from "original history" (which is limited to first-hand accounts) and from "reflective history" (which seeks to interpret the overall significance of selected events), Hegel terms his approach "philosophical history" and defines it as "nothing but the thoughtful consideration of history." In this context Hegel states the rationalistic assumption that underlies his philosophy of history, and indeed, his entire philosophic system:

> The only Thought which Philosophy brings with it to the contemplation of History, is the simple conception of *Reason;* that Reason is the Sovereign of the World; that the history of the world, therefore, presents us with a rational process. This conviction and intuition is a hypothesis in the domain of history as such. In that of Philosophy it is no hypothesis. It is there proved by speculative cognition, that Reason...is *Substance,* as well as *Infinite Power;* its own *Infinite Material* underlying all the natural and spiritual life which it originates, as also the *Infinite Form,*—that which sets this Material in motion. On the one hand, Reason is the *substance* of the Universe; viz. that by which and in which all reality has its being and subsistence. On the other hand, it is the *Infinite Energy* of the Universe; since Reason is not so powerless as to be incapable of producing anything but a mere ideal, a mere intention—having its place outside reality, nobody knows where; something separate and abstract, in the heads of certain human beings. It is the *infinite complex of things,* their entire Essence and Truth.[1]

Although it would take a great deal of space to unpack all the themes and implications of this crucial passage, special notice should be given to a few key emphases. First, there is the obvious stress upon the omnipotence of speculative Reason (with a capital 'R') as the means of ascertaining the nature and direction of human history. Next, there is the confidence that it is in fact a rational process that underlies and provides the very structure and dynamic of ultimate reality. This is the essence of Hegel's Absolute Idealism, about which more will be said shortly.

Finally, there is the explicit criticism of the interpretation of reason represented by Kant, which seeks to limit the powers of reason to the realm of phenomena. In all of these emphases one can clearly see Hegel's absolute rejection of the Kantian epistemological and ontological dichotomies.

The actual content of Hegel's philosophy of history is common knowledge. He saw history as the dialectical process by means of which the Absolute Spirit works out, and "concretizes" its own freedom and essence. On the ontological level this dialectical process takes form in relation to pure spirit, the world, and the Absolute, while on the historical level it takes form in relation to the individual, the state, and world history.[2] In another place Hegel analyzes this objectification of spirit in the historical process in terms of morality and ethics,[3] tracing the dialectical process from "law" (thesis) through "conscience" (antithesis) to "social ethics" (synthesis). In all of this Hegel's stress on the sovereignty of the rational process is never far from the center of the stage.

There is, of course, a metaphysical assumption that forms the foundation of Hegel's epistemological position—an assumption of which Hegel is aware, but for which he offers no real substantiation. Indeed, due to the nature of his system, there can be no justification of ultimate assumptions, since for Hegel "the Truth is the Whole."[4] The assumption with which he begins is simply that all reality, in spite of its many appearances to the contrary, is spiritual in essence.

> Spirit is the only Reality. It is the inner being of the world, that which essentially is, and is *per se*; it assumes objective, determinate form, and enters into relations with itself—it is externality (otherness), and exists for self; yet, in this determination, and in its otherness, it is still one with itself—it is self-contained and self-complete, in itself and for itself at once.[5]

This metaphysical position, often termed "Absolute Idealism," places Hegel squarely in the tradition of Idealism as it developed from Parmenides and Plato to Leibniz and Berkeley. He stands diametrically opposed to all forms of materialism and empiricism, and generally opposed to any form of mediating realism, such as that of Kant. Moreover, he is more akin to Parmenides than to any other idealist because of his spiritual monism, that is, his emphasis that all of reality is actually one in nature. In this way Hegel is seen to be in harmony with rationalistic idealism—à la Spinoza—rather than with empiricistic idealism, represented by Berkeley. "Everything depends upon grasping and expressing the ultimate truth not as Substance but as Subject as well."[6]

There is, however, a very important respect in which Hegel's idealism must be distinguished from positions like those of Parmenides and Spinoza. Whereas they conceived of the One in static categories, Hegel thought of the Absolute as a dialectical process that is constantly developing by setting itself over against itself, and then reuniting with itself. To oversimplify, Hegel's system might be described as something of a cross between Parmenides and Heraclitus. The spirit of reality objectifies itself by setting itself over against itself in the world (matter), and then realizes itself by uniting the spiritual and the material in the Absolute.

> True reality is merely this process of reinstating self-identity, of reflecting into its own self in and from its other, and is not an original and primal unity as such, not an immediate unity as such. It is the process of its own becoming, the circle which presupposes its end or its purpose, and has its end for its beginning; it becomes concrete and actual only by being carried out, and by the end it involves.[7]

This position of Absolute Idealism not only enabled Hegel to construct a dialectical and rationalistic epistemology in which reality is defined and understood in terms of a rational process, but it gave him the freedom to devise his own approach to the canons of human reason as well. For if ultimately Subject and Substance are one, if man's mind is identical with ultimate reality, then all the normal logical distinctions can actually be discarded. Thus in direct contradiction to the three "laws of logic," Hegel can imply that 1) everything is what it is and is also something else (contra the law of identity), 2) everything is what it is and is also its own opposite (contra the law of non-contradiction), and 3) nothing need be either what it is or its opposite (contra the law of excluded middle). The clearest example of the application of this approach is found in Part One (On Being) of Hegel's *Outlines of Logic*.[8]

On the basis of the foregoing aspects of Hegel's position, it is possible to come to grips with his understanding of religion in general and the knowledge of God in particular. First, it is essential to see that for Hegel, since ultimate reality is a monistic unity, "God" and the "Absolute" are simply different terms for the same essence. He makes this point in the following words:

> When thinking of the Absolute as subject, men have made use of statements like "God is the eternal," the "moral order of the world," or "love," etc. In such propositions ultimate truth is just barely stated to be Subject, but not set forth as the process of reflectively mediating itself within itself. In a proposition of that kind we begin with the word God. By itself this is a meaningless sound, a mere name; the predicate says afterwards what it is, gives it content and meaning; the empty beginning becomes real knowledge only when we thus get to the end of the statement. So far as that goes, why not speak alone of the etérnal, of the moral order of the world, etc., or, like the ancients, of pure conception such as being, the one, etc., i.e. of what gives the meaning without adding the meaningless sound at all? But this word just indicates that it is not a being or essence or universal in general that is put forward, but something reflected into self, a subject.[9]

Another way of expressing this ultimate unity between the Absolute (reality) and God in Hegel's thought is to say that for him philosophy and religion have the same goal and subject matter. The basic difference between philosophy and religion, at least as it is traditionally expressed, lies in their different methods. Philosophy seeks to *know* ultimate reality (the Absolute) while religion seeks to *experience* (feel) it (God). It was in this way that Hegel saw his system as the complement to, and not the enemy of, traditional religion. In fact, there was a definite sense in which Hegel's system was designed to, and actually did, become identified with the organized church of his day. "This *Good,* this *Reason,* in its most concrete form, is God. God governs the world; the actual working of his government—the carrying out of His plan—is the History of the world."[10]

It is now quite easy to see how it is that Hegel's position concerning the possibility of a knowledge of God is almost the direct antithesis of Kant's position. Where Kant claimed that speculative reason is unable, because of the categories of the mind, to provide any knowledge of ultimate reality (the noumenal world), Hegel claimed that speculative reason is able, by virtue of its ontological identity with the Absolute, to provide knowledge of ultimate reality (Spirit). After Kant had built a wall between the realms of experience and reality, Hegel proceeded to vault over that wall by means of speculative reason. Whereas Kant had said that reason is limited, Hegel said that it is unlimited.

Hegel addresses himself to the question of the knowledge of God, and explicitly rejects Kant's position:

> I have implicitly touched upon a prominent question of the day; viz. that of the possibility of knowing God: or rather—since public opinion has ceased to allow it to be a matter of *question*—the *doctrine* that it is impossible to know God. In direct contravention of what is commanded in holy Scripture as the highest duty, that we should not merely love, but *know* God,—the prevalent dogma involves the denial of what is there said; viz. that it is the Spirit (*der Geist*) that leads into Truth, knows all things, penetrates even into the deep things of the Godhead.[11]

A bit further on, Hegel states his own position in the following manner:

> In the Christian religion God has revealed Himself—that is, he has given us to understand what He is; so that He is no longer a

concealed or secret existence. And this possibility of knowing Him, thus afforded us, renders such knowledge a duty. God wishes no narrow-hearted souls or empty heads for his children; but those whose spirit is of itself indeed, poor, but rich in the knowledge of Him; and who regard this knowledge of God as the only valuable possession. That development of the thinking spirit, which has resulted from the revelation of the Divine Being as its original basis, must ultimately advance to the *intellectual conprehension* of what was presented in the first instance, to *feeling* and *imagination*.[12]

Thus Hegel not only asserts the possibility of a knowledge of God, but also the actuality of it. It should be constantly borne in mind, however, that the method and content of such knowledge are not to be found in supernatural revelation and traditional theology, but rather in speculative reasoning and philosophical theology, respectively. God is *known* by means of philosophy even though he may be *felt* by means of religion. Although he maintains that these two factors are complementary, it is obvious to even the casual reader that it is rational philosophy which is of primary importance in Hegel's system.

Despite the fact that Hegel's religious epistemology is contrary to that of Kant, there is still a definite sense in which Hegel takes Kant's position as his starting point. That is to say, it is important to remember that Hegel developed his position as a reaction to, indeed a rejection of, Kant's epistemological and ontological dichotomies. The Hegelian epistemology is an attempt to overcome Kant's dichotomies, not by reworking his basic distinctions, but by negating them. In a word, in order to provide an answer to Kant's skeptical separation of knowable phenomena and unknowable noumena, Hegel began by assuming their essential identity. But, nevertheless, Hegel plays his game within the ground rules laid out by Kant's original distinctions in that his whole system of thought is worked out in terms of overcoming them.

In the nineteenth century there were three major reactions to Hegel's system of thought. First there were those thinkers who can be classified as followers of Hegel.

These can be subdivided into two groups. On the one hand, there were those who accepted the idealistic *content* of Hegel's thought, often designated as "right-wing" Hegelians, including D. F. Strauss, A. E. Biedermann, and F. H. Bradley. On the other hand, there were those who showed a greater loyalty to the dialectical *method* within Hegel's thought and are thus designated as "left-wing" Hegelians. These thinkers nearly all became "Hegelian heretics," some of whom will be discussed presently.

A second major reaction to Hegel's system is represented in the thought of Karl Marx. His "Dialectical Materialism" began as left-wing Hegelianism and was transformed into an Hegelian heresy. Marx accepted the dialectical motif in Hegel's thought, but rejected Hegel's Idealism for a form of humanistic materialism. Following Feuerbach, who was also an Hegelian heretic, Marx maintained that the realm of proper concern is not some idealistic noumenal world, but the world of concrete human experience and activity. In this way both Feuerbach and Marx operate within the confines of the epistemological situation set forth by Kant. Marx was critical of Feuerbach, however, for interpreting the human condition in terms of subjective, inner aspirations, like love, instead of in terms of objective, external socio-economic action. It is obvious that Marx's position flatly denies any possibility of a knowledge of God, since for it no such being exists to be known.

Yet a third major reaction to Hegel's system of thought was expressed by what are today called the "existentialist" thinkers of the nineteenth century. Friedrich Nietzsche and Søren Kierkegaard were the most profound and influential progenitors of this movement. Nietzsche, as an "atheistic" existentialist, affirmed both the ridiculousness of the Absolute Idealist system *and* the meaninglessness of human existence apart from each individual's affirmation of his own meaning and worth. Kierkegaard, as a "theistic" existentialist, affirmed both the emptiness of idealistic philosophy *and* the meaninglessness of human existence *even* when the individual affirms his own meaning and worth. Kierkegaard insisted that man can find meaning only by committing himself to the Absolute (God) who has revealed himself in Christ. Whereas Nietzsche denied the possibility of a knowledge of God on the basis of the non-existence of God, Kierkegaard insisted that God can only be known by a "leap of faith" in response to Christian revelation. Thus for Kierkegaard, as well as for those who follow in his epistemological footsteps, such as Karl Barth, the wall that exists between this world and the real world because of the limits of reason—à la Kant—can be transcended only by revelation from the noumenal side. Kierkegaard accepts Kant's dichotomies, but affirms that God overcomes them through revelation and faith.

2. SCHLEIERMACHER: THE WAY OF FEELING

Another major response to the Kantian dichotomies is the work of Friedrich Schleiermacher. Both Schleiermacher and Hegel agreed that Kant's placing of the noumenal world, including God, beyond the reach of man was grossly mistaken. But whereas Hegel sought to remedy this mistake by affirming the ability of speculative reason to reflect ultimate reality, Schleiermacher sought to remedy it by affirming an altogether different avenue to the noumenal world. Kant had built his dichotomy on the assumption that the only two aspects of man's experience are thinking and doing, and since the former is limited to the phenomenal world, he concluded that if there is an avenue to God, it would have to lie in the latter. Thus he postulated a theory of religious "knowledge" based on moral activity. Schleiermacher attempted to overcome the impasse by maintaining that religious "knowledge" (in the sense of "experience") lies in a third area of human experience—namely in the area of *feeling*. In a sense Schleiermacher's approach to religious knowledge can be understood as an attempt to maintain the Christian faith in the light of Kant's critical limitation of reason. He sought to avoid this limitation by grounding religious knowledge not in cognitive reflection, but in immediate self-consciousness. Thus for Schleiermacher, the knowledge of God is a matter of experience and not a matter of reflection.

In *The Christian Faith*, which from a methodological point of view is in essential harmony with his earlier work, *On Religion: Speeches to Its Cultured Despisers*, Schleiermacher develops his experiential approach in the following way. After beginning with a confessional statement that theology must be conceived from within the church and must serve the church, he sets out to examine the nature of church community by delineating its defining characteristic. In this connection he states the major thesis that provides the foundation for his entire system: "The piety which forms the basis of all ecclesiastical communions is, considered purely in itself, neither a Knowing nor a Doing, but a modification of Feeling, or of immediate self-consciousness."[13] Before proceeding to a closer analysis of the meaning of this thesis, we should note that in focusing his attention on feeling as a characteristic of ecclesiastical community Schleiermacher has taken an anthropological starting point for his theology instead of a christological or biblical one. This point is also evident from the fact that he expressly maintains that his system must begin with propositions borrowed from ethics, philosophy of religion, and apologetics. It is, of course, this anthropological starting point which is so strongly rejected by twentieth-century "revelational" theologians like Barth, but which is the point of departure for contemporary "existentialist" theologians like Bultmann.

Schleiermacher chose the term "feeling" to call attention to an entire aspect of human experience that was simply ignored by Kant and his followers. It is in this aspect of experience that Schleiermacher locates man's awareness of God. He qualified the term "feeling" with the term "self-consciousness" in order to limit the former to those feelings of which we are consciously aware, as opposed to unconscious states. He further qualified "self-consciousness" with the term "immediate" in order to distinguish subjective and direct self-awareness from objective and rationally mediated self-awareness. Thus he wishes to locate a level of human experience midway between reflective consciousness and the unconscious. Perhaps Schleiermacher's level of feeling is similar to that presented in steam-of-consciousness novels. At any rate, he maintains that whether this self-awareness stands, as it infrequently does, in the center of our consciousness, or whether it is simply reflected, as is more often the case, in our tacit consciousness of our continuous identity, it is a real and important aspect of human life.[14]

Schleiermacher was also concerned to maintain that although feeling needs to be distinguished from knowing and doing, it must not be conceived as having no relationship to them. This is especially true in the realm of religion. On the other hand, he also wants it clearly understood that knowing and doing "only pertain to [piety] inasmuch as the stirred-up Feeling sometimes comes to rest in a thinking which fixes it, sometimes discharges itself in an action which expresses it."[15] Thus it can be seen that for Schleiermacher, feeling forms the basis or source of human experience in general, and of religious experience in particular.

Having established his anthropological, indeed psychological, starting point, Schleiermacher moved on to examine the way in which religion expresses itself in the realm of feeling. His second major thesis is this:

> The common element in all howsoever diverse expressions of piety, by which these are conjointly distinguished from all other feelings, or, in other words, the self-identical essence of piety, is this: the consciousness of being absolutely dependent, or, which is the same thing, of being in relation with God.[16]

Here then is the heart of Schleiermacher's approach to the experiential knowledge of God. Within the realm of feeling there is "an awareness of dependency," which is simply another way of saying "an awareness of God." Clearly, this thesis demands considerable analysis.

First, the word "absolute" apparently is used to designate the ultimacy of this dependence. That is to say, it is
not meant to call attention to the element of secondary, or
relative, causation of which all are aware—e.g., dependence
upon parents and food—nor to imply that there is no such
thing as relative freedom. Rather, the term "absolute" is
employed to call attention to the fact that in their immediate self-consciousness all men are aware of the radical
"whenceness" of their entire existence. "Thus in every
self-consciousness there are two elements, which we might
call respectively a self-caused element . . . and a non
self-caused element. . . , or a Being and a Having-by-some-
means-come-to-be. . . ."[17]

Second, although the awareness of "whenceness"
logically presupposes the existence of an "other" beyond
the self, "this other is not objectively presented in the
immediate self-consciousness." The move from the awareness of dependence to the affirmation of an "other" is a
reflective, or inferential, act which goes beyond the actual
experience of feeling absolutely dependent, and for this
reason will have to be dealt with a bit later. The awareness
of self and the awareness of whenceness correspond, says
Schleiermacher, to "activity" and "receptivity," respectively. All self-consciousness is composed of both of these
elements directly given in experience.

Third, and absolutely crucial, Schleiermacher claims
that this account of the nature of the feeling of absolute
dependence (as the defining characteristic of piety) must
be affirmed by both religious and nonreligious persons
alike. By this he does not mean that it must be affirmed by
all that religious persons have this feeling in common, but
that it must be affirmed by all that *all persons have this
experience in common*! Schleiermacher, indeed, says that,
"To these propositions assent can be unconditionally
demanded; and no one will deny them who is capable of a
little introspection and can find interest in the real subject
of our present inquiries."[18] Thus it is that in the *introspection* of one's feelings in general, and of one's feeling of

absolute dependence in particular, Schleiermacher seeks to establish a point of contact between all men and religion. Here is where the mystical (or intuitive) note is sounded in Schleiermacher's position. By focusing his attention upon his most immediate self-consciousness, man comes to be aware not only of his own self, but of his stark and dependent "isness." This move places man in direct contact with ultimate reality, the very "Ground of Being" itself.

Finally, Schleiermacher sets forth the sense in which he sees the awareness of absolute dependence as synonymous with being in relationship with God, and thereby lays the final plank in his attempt to construct a bridge between general human experience (phenomenal world) and experience of God (noumenal world).

> As regards the identification of absolute dependence with "relation to God" in our proposition: this is to be understood in the sense that the *Whence* of our receptive and active existence, as implied in this self-consciousness, is to be designated by the word "God," and that this is for us the really original signification of that word.[19]

To put it another way: the term "God" has been developed and used by religious persons to refer to that aspect of experience which has been isolated and designated in the foregoing analysis as "feeling of absolute dependence." And so, according to Schleiermacher, since all men are absolutely dependent upon an "other" (God), and are capable of becoming aware of their whenceness by means of introspection, it follows that such an awareness is what traditionally has been meant by being in relationship with God.

After having established his methodological starting point in the foregoing manner, Schleiermacher moved ahead to an analysis of the Christian religion and church as a particular (and highest) historical form of dependent self-consciousness. He sees it as a teleological form of monotheism, thus placing it above Judaism and Mohammedanism on the one hand and Fetishism and Polytheism on the other hand, and as unique in its exclusive focus upon the redemptive activity of Jesus Christ. In this, Schleiermacher sought to maintain the superiority of the Christian faith while at the same time maintaining the integral connection between Christianity and all forms of religion and human feeling in general.

In the course of this analysis of Christianity, Schleiermacher makes one more point of major significance for an understanding of his epistemological point of view. It is easy to see that within the context of the distinctions Schleiermacher has already made there is an implied dichotomy between religious experience and religious conceptualization. It is experience, by means of the feeling of absolute whenceness, that provides the first-hand relationship between man and God, and thus it is only appropriate to speak of *revelation* as occurring in this realm. Conceptualization, on the other hand, is a secondary and mediated way of attempting to cognize experience—and it always results in distortion. It is only in the area of conceptualization that it is proper to speak of *doctrine*.[20] Even though Schleiermacher admits that conceptualized doctrine is necessary, he adamantly insists that it is always only approximate, and must never be confused with revelation. In fact he ultimately maintains that all attempts to formulate doctrines about God are doomed to be mere negations of our own limited and dependent experience.[21] In this respect, he is similar to Kant in his skepticism about conceptual knowledge of God. However, even though theological propositions are about human self-consciousness and not about God, Schleiermacher insists that they be both relevant to the church's history and practice, and scientifically systematic. As such they must be derived from confessional documents, the New Testament, and the Old Testament (in that order), and must strive for coherence.

On the basis of these epistemological and ecclesiastical cornerstones, Schleiermacher proceeds to construct an entire theological system in which he deals with virtually every major and minor subject in the history of Christian theology. Although the content of this system is not the subject of the present study, it should be remarked that in spite of the epistemological divergence between the systems of Hegel and Schleiermacher, there is a strong convergence in their content. Schleiermacher, like Hegel, ends up with a concept of God and his relation to the world which is essentially pantheistic. Hegel drew his pantheism out of the identity between the human mind and ultimate reality by means of speculation, while Schleiermacher drew his out of the identity between human feeling and ultimate reality by means of introspection. Along with this pantheism goes a theory of causal determinism with respect to God's relation to the world.

In addition to leaving a theological legacy for the rest of the nineteenth century, in such men as Ritschl and Troeltsch, Schleiermacher's system provided the beachhead for American liberalism in the early twentieth century and for contemporary existentialist theology. Moreover, his epistemological approach bears a marked similarity to that of romanticism and philosophical existentialism as well. One man whose epistemology is almost directly parallel to Schleiermacher's is Henri Bergson. He too sought to overcome the Kantian dichotomy between phenomena and noumena by means of "tunneling under" the gulf fixed between them through the use of a direct introspection of the flow of experience. But whereas Schleiermacher focused on dependence and causality, which resulted in a pantheistic determinism, Bergson focused on process and freedom, which resulted in a creative dynamism.

Schleiermacher's position with regard to the knowledge of God can be summarized by saying that in feeling he sought an avenue of direct experience that would lead man beyond the limits of reason to an awareness of divine reality. By defining religion in terms of the feeling of absolute dependence, and Christianity as a superior modification and expression of religion, Schleiermacher sought to bring all mankind and the church together. Since all men can become aware of their absolute dependence by means of introspection, and since this is the essence of religion, it follows that all men can be religious. Moreover, since Christianity is really a modified, albeit superior, form of religion, it follows that all men can be Christian.

3. FEUERBACH: THE WAY OF NEGATION

A final major response to Kant's epistemological dichotomy, and one which is being revitalized in our own day by the "death of God" theologians, is represented in the thought of Ludwig Feuerbach. Whereas both Hegel and Schleiermacher acknowledged Kant's basic distinction between the phenomenal world and the noumenal world, and then sought to overcome it by means of speculation and introspection respectively, Feuerbach accepted the distinction and then concluded that since the noumenal world was simply a projection of the phenomenal mind, it should be dropped altogether. Feuerbach differed from Kant in that while Kant was not content to accept his own dichotomy, and hoped that it could be overcome by means of "ethical postulation," Feuerbach honestly accepted the dichotomy and refused to give the noumenal world any place in his system. In this sense, Feuerbach was more realistic and honest than any of the other thinkers who have been discussed so far.

Feuerbach's most straightforward and influential work is *The Essence of Christianity*. In the Introduction to this book he sets forth a two-fold thesis which is substantiated positively and negatively in Parts One and Two, respectively. The following summary of his position will be based upon the structure of this book.

The two-fold thesis stated in the Introduction pertains to the nature of man and the nature of religion. Feuerbach begins by locating the essence of man in his consciousness. It is his conscious, inner life which distinguishes man from all other forms of life. He shares the outward, physical dimension of life with the rest of the world, both animate and inanimate, but man alone can be aware that he is aware, man alone can choose, man alone can love.

> What, then, *is* the nature of man, of which he is conscious, or what constitutes the specific distinction, the proper humanity of man? Reason, Will, Affection. To a complete man belong the power of thought, the power of will, the power of affection. The power of thought is the light of the intellect, the power of will is energy of character, the power of affection is love. Reason, love, force of will, are perfections—the perfections of the human being—nay, more, they are absolute perfections of being. To will, to love, to think, are the highest powers, are the absolute nature of man as man, and the basis of his existence. Man exists to think, to love, to will.[22]

Moreover, Feuerbach maintains that the objects of man's consciousness, be they mental or physical, are the means by which man becomes conscious of himself and in which man's nature is reflected. "Whatever kind of object, therefore, we are at anytime conscious of, we are always at the same time conscious of our own nature; we can affirm nothing without affirming ourselves."[23] From this point Feuerbach goes on to conclude that all of man's knowledge about anything whatsoever is, in fact, the result of the activity of human consciousness. Man can know nothing, can have no experience at all, apart from it's being mediated through his own consciousness. Thus man's knowledge and reality are limited to the range of his consciousness. In a passage which sounds very much like it was taken from Kant's first *Critique,* Feuerbach states this conclusion forcefully.

> Man cannot get beyond his true nature. He may indeed by means of the imagination conceive individuals of another so-called higher kind, but he can never get loose from his species, his nature; the conditions of being, the positive final predicates which he gives to these other individuals, are always determinations or qualities drawn from his own nature—qualities in which he in truth only images and projects himself. . . . we extend our conceptions *quantitatively* not *qualitatively.*[24]

In the midst of developing this argument, Feuerbach applies his anthropomorphic principle to the question of religion and Christianity in a fashion which suggests that he was carrying on a dialogue with Schleiermacher. He takes up the theme that human feelings are the avenue of experience leading to a knowledge of God as an objective, noumenal being, and rejects it on the grounds that once one has admitted that knowledge comes by way of intro- specting one's own feelings, one has placed himself in an ego-centric predicament from which there is no escape. Feelings, like sense data in the phenomenalistic idealism of British empiricism, logically cannot function as the medi- ator of objective knowledge because they are on this side of the phenomenal-noumenal split. Thus all our knowledge is about ourselves.

> Feeling is thy own inward power, but at the same time a power distinct from thee, and independent of thee; it is in thee, above thee; it is itself that which constitutes the objec- tive in thee—thy own being which impresses thee as another being; in short, thy God. How wilt thou, then, distinguish from this objective being within thee another objective being? how wilt thou get beyond thy feeling?[25]

These considerations bring up the second part of Feuer- bach's two-fold thesis, which concerns the nature of reli- gion. If man's nature is completely determined and limited by his consciousness, then, Feuerbach concludes, all of his knowledge, whether conceptual or experiential, will be so determined and limited as well. Thus any attempt to obtain or maintain a knowledge of God will be subject to the same limitations. In Feuerbach's own words:

> Consciousness of God is self-consciousness, knowledge of God is self-knowledge. By his God thou knowest the man, and by the man his God; the two are identical. Whatever is God to a man, that is his heart and soul; and conversely, God is the manifested inward nature, the expressed self of a man,—reli- gion the solemn unveiling of a man's hidden treasures, the revelation of his intimate thoughts, the open confession of his love-secrets.[26]

Feuerbach expresses a great deal of impatience and disdain for those thinkers, such as Kant and Schleiermacher, who respond to the truth of the principle of anthropomorphism by maintaining that God cannot be described by human concepts. The *via negativa* of agnosticism or mystical pantheism is, according to Feuerbach, more irreligious and atheistic than any other position. Those who realize that all man's knowledge is self-knowledge but who go right on talking as if there were a divine being existing independently of, and indescribable by, man are the worst of deceivers.

> The denial of determinate, positive predicates concerning the divine nature is nothing else than a denial of religion, with, however, an appearance of religion in its favour, so that it is not recognized as a denial; it is simply a subtle, disguised atheism.[27]

Feuerbach asserts that an awareness of the subjectivity of religious knowledge ought, rather, to lead to an uninhibited attribution of human qualities to the divine being. The whole function of religion is to provide a concrete, flesh and blood expression of man's innermost aspirations and consciousness. "To the truly religious man, God is not a being without qualities, because to him he is a positive, real being. . . . He who earnestly believes in the Divine existence is not shocked at the attributing even of gross sensuous qualities to God."[28] Feuerbach maintains that the logical inconsistency of the *via negativa* is present as well in those thinkers who seek to construct a knowledge of God on the basis of analogy. Man simply cannot, and thus should not seek to overcome his ego-centric predicament. He should, rather, see it for what it is, and glory in it.

Another way in which Feuerbach develops his major thesis about the nature of religion is in terms of the logical relationship between subjects and predicates.

> If thou doubtest the objective truth of the predicates, thou must also doubt the objective truth of the subject whose predicates they are. If thy predicates are anthropomorphisms, the subject of them is an anthropomorphism too. If love, goodness, personality, etc., are human attributes, so also is the

subject which thou presupposest, the existence of God, the belief that there is a God, an anthropomorphism—a presupposition purely human.[29]

Feuerbach substantiates his account of the nature of religion by appealing to two facts established by the empirical study of religion. First, it can be conclusively shown that the concept of God in all of the varying instances and levels of religious societies always reflects the self-consciousness and aspirations of the people in that society. Witness the relationship between the Homeric gods and the Greek mind, between Odin and the ancient Germanic peoples, and between Jehovah and the early Hebrews. Second, the more any particular religion or person seeks to deny man's identity with God, the more the nature of man is depreciated. The same is true when this contrast is inverted so as to stress the importance of man to the depreciation of God. Feuerbach cites the Augustinian-Pelagian controversy as an example of this principle. If man's concept of God were not a projection of his own nature, Feuerbach argues, this polar relationship between the appreciation and depreciation of God and man would not obtain.

The conclusion of all of these considerations is stated by Feuerbach in unequivocal terms: "Man—this is the mystery of religion—projects his being into external objectivity, and than again makes himself an object to this projected image of himself thus converted into a subject...."[30]

The rest of Feuerbach's position follows naturally from his two-fold thesis about the nature of man and religion. In Part One of *The Essence of Christianity* Feuerbach takes up the major doctrines of Christianity one by one, and attempts to demonstrate how they are, in fact, really reflections of human consciousness. He titles this part "The True or Anthropological Essence of Religion," and takes up such doctrines as the nature of God, the Trinity, the Incarnation, creation, prayer, faith, miracles, Christ, and Heaven. Perhaps two quotations will serve to illustrate how Feuerbach applies his two-fold thesis:

On God:

> Of all the attributes which the understanding assigns to God, that which in religion, and especially in the Christian religion, has the pre-eminence, is moral perfection. But God as a morally perfect being is nothing else than the realised idea, the fulfilled law of morality, the moral nature of man posited as the absolute being.[31]

On the Incarnation:

> God, for the sake of man, empties himself of his Godhead, lays aside his Godhead. Herein lies the elevating influence of the Incarnation; the highest, the perfect being humiliates, lowers himself for the sake of man. Hence in God I learn to estimate my own nature; I have value in the sight of God; the divine significance of my nature is become evident to me.[32]

Part One concludes:

> Our most essential task is now fulfilled. We have reduced the supermundane, supernatural, and superhuman nature of God to the elements of human nature as its fundamental elements. Our process of analysis has brought us again to the position with which we set out. The beginning, middle and end of religion is MAN.[33]

Part Two, titled "The False or Theological Essence of Religion," seeks to show that when the anthropomorphic nature of religion is ignored, the doctrines of Christianity become self-contradictory. Feuerbach maintains that the concept of a perfect being existing independently of human experience is contradictory on two counts. First, as Kant had shown, the arguments for the existence of such a being are all fallacious because they seek to transcend the limits of reason. Second, the very concept of a perfect being is self-negating, since perfection is simply the negation of human imperfection. From all this it follows that the ideas of a divine revelation, of Sacraments, and of faith, as involving the activity of a being external to man, are all seen to be without substance.

Now it is of paramount importance to see that Feuerbach conceived of his position as making the ultimate
positive contribution to the proper understanding and
appreciation of religion. He saw himself as a prophetic
theologian whose task was to call Christianity back to its
real nature and area of concern. Only when the mask and
myth of objectivism and hypostatization had been torn
away could religion and humanity see themselves for what
they are, and unite in their common task: the appreciation
and development of man. As Feuerbach says in his preface:

> Religion is the dream of the human mind. But even in dreams
> we do not find ourselves in emptiness or in heaven, but on
> earth, in the realm of reality; we only see real things in the
> entrancing splendour of imagination and caprice, instead of in
> the simple daylight of reality and necessity. Hence I do
> nothing more to religion—and to speculative philosophy and
> theology also—than to open its eyes, or rather to turn its gaze
> from the internal towards the external, i.e., I change the object
> as it is in the imagination into the object as it is in reality.[34]

Thus it is that Feuerbach's response to the Kantian
epistemological situation is best understood as one of
negation. Feuerbach accepts Kant's dichotomy as final,
something which Kant himself seemed unable to do, and
then in the fashion of Occam slices away the whole idea of
a transcendent, noumenal world as both contradictory and
insidious. Standing before the wall he had constructed
between the phenomenal and noumenal worlds, Kant re-
mained hopeful that the noumenal world, including God,
was real. Hegel and Schleiermacher, on the other hand,
sought to climb over or dig under the wall. Feuerbach
simply turned his back on the whole question and gave his
attention to the phenomenal world.

The nineteenth-century thinker most similar to Feuerbach is Auguste Comte. There are, of course, wide differences between them, but both begin and end with Man.
Comte also accepted Kant's dichotomy and concluded that
the business of philosophy was to promote the full-scale

application of human reason, as contained in the scientific method, to the social dimension of the phenomenal world. This concern with the social realm marks the sharpest difference between Comte and Feuerbach, although both agree that a concern for the noumenal world is completely fruitless. Comte, the acknowledged father of positivism and sociology, was concerned to overcome the lag of society and culture behind science and technology by applying the scientific method to the study of, and the reformation of, man's social and cultural relationships. In this way he sought the unification of all human knowledge.

According to Comte this process of unification has three progressive stages. First there is the "theological stage," in which man understands his world in terms of gods, evil powers, and black magic. In this primitive stage everything is anthropomorphized and one gets along by "bribing" nature and one's fellowman. Second there is the "metaphysical stage," in which man understands himself in terms of ordered patterns and rational processes which still have their ground in the noumenal world. In this transitional stage (represented by the modern Western world) man develops the distinction between what *is* and what *ought* to be. That is, ethics is born. Finally, there is the "positive stage" (on the threshold of which mankind stood in the nineteenth century) in which there is no attempt to explain the facts of this world by reference to anything outside of this world. The facts of human experience provide the norm for all judgments. In this ultimate society, religion is interpreted in terms of working for the good of humanity, both now and in the future. The need for a commitment to a cause other than oneself is basic, but should be directed to man's social well-being and not to something transcendental:

> In the final, the positive state, the mind has given over the vain search after Absolute notions, the origin and destination of the universe, and the causes of phenomena, and applies itself to the study of their laws—that is, their invariable relations of

succession and resemblance. Reasoning and observation, duly combined, are the means of this knowledge. What is now understood when we speak of an explanation of facts is simply the establishment of a connection between single phenomena and some general facts, the number of which continually diminishes with the progress of science. [35]

Throughout this survey of nineteenth-century thought I have maintained that its various thinkers and emphases are best understood as diverging responses to the Kantian dichotomy. In this way I have sought to establish the claim that, to a large extent, the epistemological dualism which lies at the base of contemporary thought was inherited from the nineteenth century. Although nearly every twentieth-century philosophical and theological movement has thrown over the positions developed in the nineteenth century, none of them have sought to rework the Kantian ground rules within which those positions were constructed. Some contemporary emphases seek to circumvent the nineteenth century by going directly back to Kant. What is really needed, however, is a position which goes behind and then beyond Kant. But we cannot begin to undermine Kant's dichotomized epistemology until we have presented and analyzed it. This will be the task of the next chapter.

III: Locating the Source: Immanuel Kant

In the preceding chapters I have argued that contemporary philosophy is characterized by intellectual segregation, the empiricists and existentialists standing against one another, but that in spite of this ideological bifurcation, there is an essential unity underlying the contemporary scene. Divergent and opposed as these two major movements are, they agree that a qualitative distinction must be made between the two main areas of human experience and reality. This distinction is variously expressed as between science and morality, fact and value, cognitivity and nonsense, knowledge and mystery. The empiricists maintain that only that aspect of reality and experience which can be conceptualized and empirically confirmed is of real significance. The existentialists maintain that only that aspect of reality and experience which deals with human emotions and values is of real significance.

This divided-but-united situation is reflected in the contemporary discussion of the question of religious knowledge. Both confessionally oriented theologians (following in the Barthian tradition) and existentially oriented theologians (following the Bultmannian tradition) work under the assumption that religious awareness and conceptual cognitivity are essentially distinct. The "infinite qualitative distinction" between knowledge and faith which pervades Kierkegaard's thought continues to dominate the contemporary scene. Moreover, as I tried to indicate in the second chapter, this basic agreement on the hiatus between these two main aspects of human experience also dominated the thought of philosophers and theologians in the nineteenth century.

The purpose of the present chapter is to make a case for the essential similarity, if not historical causality, between the philosophy of Immanuel Kant and this dominant characteristic of modern thought. Here again, special attention will be given to the possibility of religious knowledge. But first some preliminary matters.

1. FORERUNNERS: PLATO AND HUME

My purpose is not to argue that Kant was the only or even the first influential thinker to suggest a dichotomy between the cognitive and non-cognitive realms of reality or experience. Obviously there were others before him who helped to develop the position. My contention is that in the thought of Kant this dualism is expressed in an especially precise and far-reaching fashion. Kant drew the lines for this dichotomy in a way which has not been equalled in pointedness and profundity. In order to better understand Kant's position, however, it may be helpful to review briefly certain aspects of the thought of two philosophers who also proposed, or implied, such a dichotomy.

Plato is often taken to be the forefather of classical rationalism or idealism, in which the term "knowledge" applies in the strict sense only to an awareness of ultimate reality (the Forms). There are, of course, many passages in Plato's writings which do seem to support this interpretation, an interpretation clearly implying a dichotomy between "temporary" and "eternal" knowledge which in some ways parallels the dichotomy with which I am concerned. Yet, closer study indicates that Plato's view is actually closer to the position constructed by Hegel, in that both philosophers opt for a type of cognitivity transcending all distinctions.

Moreover, a very strong case can be made for an interpretation of Plato which sees him as constructing a view of knowledge more flexible and less "inflationary" than that discussed above. The "divided line" passage in Book VI of *The Republic* seems to imply several levels of knowledge, and the later dialogues seem to conclude that the criterion of causing or being subject to change makes room in reality for "becoming" as well as "being." Thus the Forms are not the only reality and knowledge of them is not the only knowledge. Rather there is a continuum of degrees of knowledge corresponding to a continuum of degrees of reality.

Without exploring these interpretations, I would like to examine an aspect of Plato's philosophy which does clearly point to a split between the realms of fact and value. How this aspect of his thought relates to the foregoing interpretations I will leave to the Plato scholars. The part of Plato's thought I have in mind is his infamous attack upon the arts in Book X of *The Republic*.

As is well known, Plato maintains that the arts, especially painting, poetry, and drama, are to be eliminated from, or at least strongly controlled within, the ideal society. The reasons for this strong position seem to be two in number. First, the arts are inferior to philosophy or science because to the extent that they seek to represent reality they fail; the objects or persons they portray are themselves only copies (images) of Formal Reality. Thus the works of art are actually twice removed from reality—and hence from truth as well—because they are copies of copies. Second, inasmuch as the arts do not represent reality, they must be viewed as appealing to man's emotions. Since Plato's view of human nature involves a rather clear-cut division between the emotions, the will, and the mind, with the emotions' needing to be held in check by the mind, he concludes that anything which seeks to stir up the emotions without appealing first to the mind can only be subversive, both to the individual and to the state.

We have, then, a fair case against the poet and we may set him down as the counterpart of the painter, whom he resembles in two ways: his creations are poor things by the standard of truth and reality, and his appeal is not to the highest part of the soul, but to one which is equally inferior. So we shall be justified in not admitting him into a well-ordered commonwealth, because he stimulates and strengthens an element which threatens to undermine the reason. As a country may be given over into the power of its worst citizens while the better sort are ruined, so, we shall say, the dramatic poet sets up a vicious form of government in the individual soul: he gratifies that senseless part which cannot distinguish great and small, but regards the same things as now one, now the other; and he is an image-maker whose images are phantoms far removed from reality.[1]

Plato's criticism of the arts entails a fact-value dichotomy very much like that which characterizes contemporary thought. Each of his reasons for rejecting the arts as inadequate presupposes such a split. The first reason assumes that all knowledge is representational and not creative in function, while the second assumes that all knowledge is mental and not emotional in nature. In each case Plato seems dangerously close to becoming the forerunner of positivism! He clearly maintains a dualism between the cognitive and non-cognitive realms of experience.

But there is another emphasis in Plato's thought which counteracts this dualism, and which might well serve as a clue to the way in which it can be overcome. I have in mind the fact that Plato holds that the Forms of moral reality are as capable of being known as are the other Forms. This emphasis argues against a dichotomy between fact and value by insisting that both are knowable, or cognitive in nature. However, it is extremely difficult, if not impossible to synthesize Plato's diverse emphases, and thus it must be acknowledged that at least some of them contribute to the development of an epistemological dualism.

In the main, Plato can be said to represent the cognitive side of the cognitive-non-cognitive dichotomy. The other side has been represented throughout Western thought by the mystical tradition, from Plotinus and pseudo-Dionysius to Meister Eckhart. Such thinkers have denied that the mystical knowledge of God is cognitive. In this way they have opposed men like Augustine, who followed in the tradition of Plato. Nevertheless, both sides have tended to hold that reality or experience must be divided into two main parts. They have disagreed over the part to which the awareness of God is to be related. It was not until modern times, however, that this epistemological dualism came on the scene with full force.

Although Descartes, Leibniz, Hobbes, and Locke all addressed themselves to this issue in one way or another, it was left for David Hume to place it at center stage. In fact it was from Hume that Kant inherited his philosophical problems. Having been thoroughly schooled in, and convinced of, the rationalistic views of Leibniz and Wolff, Kant was rudely awakened from his "dogmatic slumber" by the profundity of Hume's thought.

Hume put an end to the high hopes of both the continental rationalists and the British empiricists. The former sought and claimed to have found an epistemological foundation for all knowledge in the necessary conclusions deducible from self-evident truths. The latter sought and claimed to have found such a foundation in the probable conclusions "inducible" from sense impressions. Hume followed the empiricist approach more rigorously than his predecessors and argued a convincing case that neither deduction nor induction can provide an adequate foundation for knowledge. Deduction, with its "self-evident" premises, turned out to be definitional (analytic) and empty of factual content, while induction proved to be based upon the indemonstrable assumption that the future must be like the past. Thus Hume thought he had eliminated the possibility of factual truth-claims in mathematics, science, and metaphysics.

Beginning with the position that the objects of human consciousness ("perceptions") are either sensory impressions or ideas of such impressions, Hume arrived at the following conclusion:

> All the objects of human reason or inquiry may naturally be divided into two kinds, to wit, *relations of ideas* and *matters of fact*. Of the first kind are the sciences of geometry, algebra, and arithmetic; and in short, every affirmation which is either intuitively or demonstratively certain. . . . Propositions of this kind are discoverable by the mere operation of thought, without dependence on what is anywhere existent in the universe. . . . Matters of fact, which are the second objects of human reason, are not ascertained in the same manner; nor is our evidence of their truth, however great, of a like nature with the foregoing. The contrary of every matter of fact is still possible; because it can never imply a contradiction. . . .[2]

It is quite obvious that here in Hume's thought lie the beginnings of what today is known as logical empiricism. The distinction between logical and empirical knowledge serves as the foundational stone of contemporary empiricism, as was brought out in Chapter One. Hume continued his epistemological inquiry by arguing that since no rational basis can be found for causal or inductive inference, the knowledge claim inherent in factual assertions is bogus. In spite of his skeptical conclusions, however, Hume did acknowledge that causal inference when applied to empirical experience has a firm basis in psychological association, reinforced by the constant repetition of instances. Thus he concludes his inquiry with a strong dichotomy between those areas of human concern which are worthy of study (cognitive) and those which are not (noncognitive):

> When we run over libraries, persuaded of these principles, what havoc must we make? If we take in our hand any volume; of divinity or school metaphysics, for instance; let us ask, Does it contain any abstract reasoning concerning quantity or number? No. Does it contain any experimental reasoning concerning matter of fact and existence? No. Commit it then to the flames: for it can contain nothing but sophistry and illusion.[3]

Another place where the dichotomized nature of Hume's position is clearly evident is in the logical gap which he insists exists between statements involving "is" and those involving "ought." In brief, Hume maintains that statements of moral discourse have nothing whatever to do with statements of factual discourse. Here again, one can see the core of logical empiricism and the dichotomy between fact and value upon which it is based.

> But can there be any difficulty in proving that vice and virtue are not matters of fact, whose existence we can infer by reason? Take any action allowed to be vicious; wilful murder, for instance. Examine it in all lights, and see if you can find that matter of fact, or real existence, which you call *vice*. In whichever way you take it, you find only certain passions, motives, volitions, and thoughts. There is no other matter of fact in the case. The vice entirely escapes you, as long as you consider the object. You never can find it, till you turn your reflection into your own breast, and find a sentiment of disapprobation, which arises in you, towards this action. Here is a matter of fact; but it is the object of feeling, not of reason. It lies in yourself, not in the object.[4]

In spite of the obvious indications of the existence of a fact-value dichotomy in the thought of such earlier thinkers as Plato and Hume, it remains the case that this dichotomy obtains precise and thorough treatment only in the work of Kant. The rest of this present chapter will be devoted to an analysis of the nature and implications of Kant's position, with an eye to locating it as the source of the dichotomy which plagues modern thought.

2. KANT AND RELIGIOUS KNOWLEDGE[5]

Kant was convinced of the validity of Hume's reasoning, but at the same time was aware that mathematical, scientific, and metaphysical knowledge form a vital part of the human situation, and seem to be quite well established. The question which serves as the focal point of Kant's philosophy is this: How are mathematical, scientific and metaphysical knowledge possible? In other words, since such knowledge is a reality, what must be the case in order to account for its existence? The answer which he worked out not only serves as a synthesis of rationalism and empiricism, but represents a profound epistemological revolution which Kant himself likened to Copernicus' astronomical revolution.

Kant's epistemology, set forth in his *Critique of Pure Reason*, is based on the belief that knowledge is composed of two aspects, namely content and form. With the empiricists he maintains that the content of knowledge is supplied by sensory experience, but in harmony with rationalism he maintains that the form (or structure) of knowledge is supplied by the mind. Kant asserted that the mind plays an active part in the knowing experience by imposing upon the data of sensation certain fixed "categories." Thus what is known is sensory experience after it has been "filtered through," or organized by, the built-in categories of the understanding. Both of these elements are necessary, but neither is sufficient, for knowledge to exist.

> But though all our knowledge begins with experience, it does not follow that it all arises out of experience. For it may well be that even our empirical knowledge is made up of what we receive through impressions and of what our own faculty of knowledge (sensible impressions serving merely as the occasion) supplies from itself. If our faculty of knowledge makes any such addition, it may be that we are not in a position to distinguish it from the raw material, until with long practice of attention we have become skilled in separating it.[6]

Although no sensations of these categories are possible, we do possess "ideas" of them. The concepts of space, time, and causation are perhaps the most crucial and will have to suffice as examples in this brief discussion. Concepts such as these are common and essential in ordinary and theoretic understanding, and yet they have no content of their own, i.e., they cannot be perceived. Rather, according to Kant, they are the very framework by means of which objects can be experienced and understood. Moreover, because of their all-pervasive, categorical nature, these concepts can be said to yield necessary (*a priori*) and factual (*synthetic*) knowledge.[7] All human experience and knowledge must be characterized by space, time, causation, etc., since these comprise the very nature of the human mind. Thus statements involving these concepts can be both necessarily true and factually significant.

This necessary-factual, or *a priori-synthetic*, knowledge provides an answer, according to Kant, to the crucial question of how knowledge is possible. Mathematical knowledge and scientific knowledge find their basis and justification in the categories of the understanding, since the latter are the necessary conditions of human thought. Geometry, which is dependent upon the category of space, and arithmetic, which is dependent upon the category of time (sequence), yield a knowledge which is necessary, but *not* empty of factual content. In like manner, science, which is dependent upon the category of causation as the basis of inductive inference, yields a knowledge which guarantees that future experiences will follow a causal pattern similar to that of past experiences. Kant was convinced that *a priori-synthetic* knowledge, based on the categories of the understanding, provides a thorough and final answer to the problems raised by Hume.

To put the whole matter another way, Hume had maintained that 1) all statements that are known to be true apart from experience (*a priori*) are also analytic (definitional); 2) all statements that have factual content (synthetic) are known to be true only on the basis of experience (*a posteriori*); therefore 3) all significant statements are either *a priori*-analytic or *a posteriori*-synthetic; and finally 4) since *a priori*-analytic statements make no factual claims and *a posteriori*-synthetic statements unjustifiably assume causal inference, knowledge claims are without complete rational justification. Kant, on the other hand, replied that since the categories of the understanding are necessary to explain the fact of human knowledge, and since these categories yield concepts which are both necessary and factually significant, there must exist *a priori-*

synthetic statements which provide a sound basis for knowledge claims.

One example of an *a priori*-synthetic statement is all that can be given in this brief survey of Kant's thought. This example is one of Kant's favorites. The mathematical proposition $7 + 5 = 12$ is both necessarily true and factually significant, since its truth can be determined apart from experience (*a priori*), but it actually says something about the world of experience (synthetic). It is not analytic, since 12 is not part of one's mental conception when one thinks or says $7 + 5$, and it is not *a posteriori*, since truth is not dependent upon the experience of actually counting objects. $7 + 5 = 12$ is *a priori*-synthetic because it is based upon the mental category of sequence (time). The serious logical shortcomings of Kant's understanding of mathematics will have to be overlooked in this exposition.

Kant's account of metaphysics does not conclude with the same positive results as his account of mathematics and science. Since both mathematics and science are attempts to conceptualize about the world of sensory experience (phenomena), their use of the categories of the understanding is quite appropriate. The results of the application of these categories to the phenomenal world are reliable because the phenomenal world actually derives its reality from the categories in the first place. Metaphysics, however, is traditionally defined as the study of reality as it really is (noumena), apart from the limitations of sensory experience—the study of reality in and of itself (*ding an sich*). In such an endeavor, it is clear that the application of the categories of the mind would be completely inappropriate, since these phenomenal categories would distort one's understanding of the noumena in the same way that dark green sunglasses distort one's perception of color. But if these categories of the understanding, which comprise the human intellect, cannot be used in metaphysics, what categories can be used? Clearly none, for these are the only mental categories man has at his disposal. Man's knowledge is limited by the nature of his intellect. Thus Kant con-

cludes that metaphysics, as it has traditionally been conceived, is strictly impossible:

> Therefore all concepts, and with them all principles, even such
> as are possible *a priori*, relate to empirical intuitions, that is, to
> the data for a possible experience. Apart from this relation
> they have no objective validity, and in respect of their repre-
> sentations are a mere play of imagination or of under-
> standing.[8]

Kant devotes a good deal of space to a discussion of the
mistakes and confusions which result from the abortive
attempt to transcend the categories of the understanding
by conceptualizing about the noumenal world.[9] Instead of
transcending the categories, one actually ends up applying
them to themselves, which in turn results in either empty
abstractions or anthropomorphic hypostatizations. The
history of philosophy is replete with examples of both.
Kant mentions three such mistakes, and classifies them as
"The Psychological Idea," "The Cosmological Idea," and
"The Theological Idea."[10] The first is a result of applying
the category of "substance" to the noumena in order to
obtain the concept of a soul, or self. The second is a result
of applying the category of "causation" to the noumena in
order to construct a concept of the world. The third
results from applying the category of "possibility and
necessity" to the noumena by way of constructing a concept of God.

It is on the basis of the inapplicability of the categories
of the mind to the noumenal world that Kant develops his
profound criticisms of the traditional arguments for God's
existence. The ontological and causal arguments are im-
potent because they attempt to arrive at conclusions about
reality beyond the phenomenal world by means of the
categories of phenomenal knowledge and experience. Thus
they become pure abstractions, empty of factual (existential, in the logical sense) content. There are, of course,
other logical reasons which Kant offers in criticism of such
arguments, but this is not the place to review them. Kant
states his conclusion thus:

> Now I maintain that all attempts to employ reason in theology in any merely speculative manner are altogether fruitless and by their very nature null and void, and that the principles of its employment in the study of nature do not lead to any theology whatsoever. Consequently, the only theology of reason which is possible is that which is based upon moral laws or seeks guidance from them. All synthetic principles of reason allow only of an immanent employment; and in order to have knowledge of a supreme being we should have to put them to a transcendent use, for which our understanding is in no way fitted.[11]

Traditional metaphysics is, then, impossible. Nevertheless, Kant realized that thinkers will continually be tempted to apply their reasoning powers beyond their limits, and that the "metaphysical urge" is here to stay. To cope with these two facts, Kant offered two suggestions. First, he wrote a shortened and simplified version of his epistemological analysis entitled, *Prolegomena To Any Future Metaphysics*, in which he advised thinkers not to bother themselves with traditional metaphysics, since it is a strict, logical impossibility. Second, he proposed that the term "metaphysics" be "recoined" so as to refer to the analysis of the nature and limitations of human thought—following Kant's own example:

> Critique, therefore, and critique alone contains in itself the whole well-proved and well-tested plan, and even all the means, required to establish metaphysics as a science; by other ways and means it is impossible.[12]

I turn now to Kant's account of morality as set forth in his *Critique of Practical Reason*. The type of reasoning employed in matters of ethics is not speculative (with conceptual understanding as its goal), but rather it is practical (with moral action as its goal).[13] Although this reasoning is not subject to conceptual categories, it is subject to the categorical imperative of duty. Every man is confronted with the imperative, "Do your duty," and whether a particular decision is moral or immoral is determined solely on the basis of whether or not it was made in response to this call of duty. For Kant, an imperative to do one's duty necessarily implies the freedom to be able to do one's duty. It was upon this foundation of personal freedom that Kant built his entire system of moral and educational excellence.

The line Kant drew between pure (speculative) and practical (moral) reason was clear and impassable. There were at least two important reasons for drawing the line in this way. First, it enabled Kant to isolate and thus delimit the nature and limitations of speculative reason. Second, it enabled Kant to establish moral philosophy and action on an independent and autonomous basis. Others had suggested similar distinctions before him, but none had worked out the dichotomy between fact and value so thoroughly. Here is the cornerstone of nearly all of contemporary philosophy and theology: "The theoretical use of reason was concerned with objects of the cognitive faculty only. . . . It is quite different with the practical use of reason. In this, reason is concerned with the grounds of determination of the will. . . ."[14]

Kant's account of religion, not surprisingly, fits smoothly into the epistemological and moral dichotomy outlined in the foregoing discussion. Traditionally, religion had found its basis in the realm of knowledge, and more particularly in the field of metaphysics. The claims of religion were construed as knowledge claims about ultimate (noumenal) reality. This approach not only led to insoluble conflicts between interpretations (Kant called them "antinomies"), but it left religion open to the criticisms of logic and science. By delineating the phenomenal limits of knowledge claims, Kant rendered this view of religion entirely sterile. The end of metaphysics meant the end of religious speculation. But far from considering himself the enemy of religion, Kant conceived of himself as its chief benefactor. By making a thorough and clear distinction between speculative reason and practical reason, he had provided religion with a basis in the moral realm, which not only moved it out of range of intellectual criticism, but allowed it to focus on its primary business as well. Religion's main concerns are, according to Kant, obeying God and serving mankind, and these have to do with morality, not knowledge.

Although his *Critiques* make some mention of this conclusion,[15] Kant worked out its implications most thoroughly in his *Religion Within the Limits of Reason Alone*. Here he distinguishes between a reasoned and a revealed religion. The former is based on practical reason and is primarily concerned with morality, while the latter is based on historical facts and is primarily concerned with doctrines and practices. Only the former can be universal, since it is based on the moral imperative which every man experiences, while the latter is based on special information which is limited to a few. One of the main concerns of Kant's *Religion* is to develop the relationship between his moral religion within the limits of practical reason and the Christian religion set forth in Scripture. He maintained that when men

> fulfil their duties to men (themselves and others) they are, by these very acts, performing God's commands and are therefore in all their actions and abstentions, so far as these concern morality, perpetually in the service of God, and that it is absolutely impossible to serve God more directly in any other way (since they can affect and have an influence upon earthly beings alone, and not upon God).[16]

It is precisely at this point that the connection between Kant's position and contemporary theology as discussed in Chapter One can be seen most clearly. Up to the point where he concludes the negative phase of his argument, Kant provides an unequivocal foundation for the thought of both Barth and Bultmann. Both of the dominant theological movements of our day reject any attempts to base religion and theology upon speculative reason. However, when Kant goes ahead to reject revelation as the basis of religion, he parts company with the main thrust of Barth's thought. On the other hand, when he places religion in the moral realm, he continues to perform as a forerunner, along with Kierkegaard, of Bultmann's position.

Essentially the same relationship as the above exists between Kant's thought and that of the dominant movements of contemporary philosophy. Both empiricism and existentialism reject classical metaphysical philosophy as impossible. And although both of these movements also reject Kant's notion of *a priori*-synthetic knowledge, existentialism is in agreement with the positive development of Kant's thought to the degree that it (existentialism) separates the valuational realm from the factual. Kant clearly emerges, then, as the intellectual progenitor of the contemporary dichotomized situation in both theology and philosophy.

One final point remains to be discussed in this survey of Kant's thought. Once having separated knowledge and morality, and having identified religion with the latter, Kant allowed himself to conjecture about the implications of his view of religion. I have already mentioned that he was convinced that the imperative nature of moral duty implies individual freedom. In addition, Kant maintained that the moral imperative of duty "implies" personal immortality and the existence of God.[17] Since man is faced with the moral imperative to become a person who does his duty, in short a virtuous person, it is only reasonable (from a practical standpoint) to "postulate" the continuation of life after death and the existence of an eternal, all-good God. Immortality is necessary to allow sufficient time to achieve the desired virtue, and God is necessary to serve as the ground and standard of the desired virtue. Beginning with the experiential fact of moral responsibility, Kant reasoned to the opportunity for its fulfillment (immortality) and the Judge (God) to make it a reality. If a man is to be held responsible, he must be provided with the opportunity for achievement, and there must be a source and standard of achievement.

> . . .a requirement of pure *practical* reason is based on a *duty*, that of making something (the *summum bonum*) the object of my will so as to promote it with all my powers; in which case I must suppose its possibility and, consequently, also the condi-

tions necessary thereto, namely, God, freedom, and immortality. . . . But the subjective effect of this law, namely, the mental *disposition* conformed to it and made necessary by it, to promote the practically possible *summum bonum*, this pre-supposes at least that the latter is *possible*, for it would be practically impossible to strive after the object of a conception which at bottom was empty and had no object.[18]

This is Kant's famous "moral argument" for the reality of God and immortality. I use the terms "imply," "necessitate," and "argument" in a qualified sense. In no sense did Kant think of these considerations as rational demonstrations. Nonetheless, he did view them as practical implications of the moral life which establish the reality of religion in the only way it can and needs to be established. It is in this way that Kant claimed to have "found it necessary to deny *knowledge* in order to make room for *faith*."[19]

3. THE PROSECUTION RESTS

The case against Kant as the primary source of the profoundly influential and insidious dichotomy between fact and value is almost complete. All that remains to be added to the case against Kant is the testimony of several contemporary philosophers who also interpret him as proposing the dichotomy we have discussed.

In his excellent book on Kant's first *Critique*, P. F. Strawson traces Kant's argument against applying the categories of the understanding to the noumenal world under the heading "The Logic of Illusion." After discussing the concepts of the soul, the cosmos, and God, Strawson addresses himself to "The Illusions of Philosophical Theology." He concludes with the following remarks:

> The case against a theology based on the theoretical employment of reason is concluded. Neither by *a priori* nor by empirical arguments can the existence of a divine being be established. "The only theology of reason which is possible is that which is based upon moral laws or seeks guidance from them." Nevertheless a thorough understanding of the neces-

sary incompetence of theoretical reason in this sphere is not without a twofold negative utility to theology itself. If we are inhibited from asserting, we are also inhibited from denying, on theoretical grounds, what we may have other, perhaps moral, grounds for accepting; and we are restrained from importing empirical impurities into any conception of an ideal being in which a moral theology may give us grounds for belief.[20]

Similarly, George F. Thomas finds in the rigid dualisms between phenomena and noumena, sensation and understanding, theoretical and practical reason the source of major difficulties in Kant's philosophy. More specifically, Thomas pinpoints the difficulties connected with Kant's denial of the possibility of knowledge of God in terms of Kant's dichotomy between pure and practical reason. In addition to being inhibited from constructing a religious epistemology by his disenchantment with the systematic theology of his day,

> Kant was also inhibited by his *dualism* between *theoretical* and *practical reason.* The distinction between the theoretical and the practical functions of reason is a real one, and it is as old as Aristotle. But Kant misconceives these functions when he limits the theoretical reason to *cognition of objects* and the practical reason to *legislation for action.* The effect of this sharp division of functions is a dualism of what *is* and what *ought to be,* existence and value. Once this dualism has arisen, it is difficult to overcome it.[21]

It was my reading several years ago of John E. Smith's discussion of Kant's relation to the possibility of religious knowledge which first suggested to me that Kant is the source of the contemporary stalemate. Smith argues, as I have done, that Kant's dualism not only leads to severe epistemological difficulties, but has undermined the possibility of constructing an adequate and comprehensive theory of the knowledge of God:

> If we survey the development of religious thought since Kant, we cannot escape one fact: Most thinkers who have taken Kant as a point of departure have accepted without question the validity of the analysis through which he arrived at his

> conclusions regarding the limitation of reason. . . . We need to
> ask whether there is any rational way out of the impasse in the
> present philosophical and religious situation: On one side
> stands the domain of "factual" knowledge represented by
> science and positivistic philosophies and on the other stands
> "value" represented by existential philosophies and theology.
> The existence of this split in the modern intellectual situation
> points back to the ultimate dualism in Kant's own thought.
> . . .[22]

The witness of these three thinkers corroborates the
claims of my first three chapters in general and those of
this present chapter in particular. Smith points specifically
to the need to ask the question of whether there is any
way out of the impasse whose results are clearly evident in
contemporary thought and whose source is to be found in
Kant's epistemology. It is precisely this question which I
have tried to raise in these chapters. The attempt to
construct an answer will provide the focus of the chapters
yet to come.

Nowhere are the rigidity, frustration, and pessimism of
Kant's epistemological dualism more forcefully expressed
than in his own writings. Speaking of the cognitive
domain, Kant says:

> This domain is an island, enclosed by nature itself within
> unalterable limits. It is the land of truth—enchanting name!—
> surrounded by a wide and stormy ocean, the native home of
> illusion, where many a fog bank and many a swiftly melting
> iceberg give the deceptive appearance of farther shores, de-
> luding the adventurous seafarer ever anew with empty hopes,
> and engaging him in enterprises which he can never abandon
> and yet is unable to carry to completion.[23]

To conclude, let me summarize the main reasons I take
the epistemological dualism epitomized by Kant's position
to be so very unfortunate. To begin with, as has been
stressed throughout these three chapters, the epistemological dualism based on a dichotomy between fact and
value has led to an exceedingly frustrating stalemate between empiricism and existentialism. The foundation upon
which both of these movements rest makes it impossible to

consolidate their respective insights. Not only does this fact render dialogue between empiricism and existentialism next to impossible, it also creates profound discontent for anyone who is drawn to both points of view.

Secondly, this dichotomy is simply contrary to the structure of everyday experience and language. The fact is that persons neither receive nor respond to experience as if it were divided into factual and valuational components. Persons experience and respond as holistic units, without constantly "shifting gears" between matters of fact and matters of value. The contexts of decision and judgment always involve cognitive and non-cognitive factors in inextricable combination. We do not and cannot separate our talk about what "is" from our talk about what "ought" to be. When a theory of knowledge is out of harmony with the practice of knowledge, then the theory stands in need of overhaul.

Finally, the dualism following from Kant's dichotomies leads to an extremely unhappy dilemma. Given Kant's distinctions and the contemporary scene, one is forced to choose between the domains of fact and value in seeking a basis for his philosophy of life. This dilemma is especially acute with respect to the question of the knowledge of God. Once religious knowledge is located on the value side of the epistemological gap, one is forced to choose between equally unacceptable alternatives. If, in order to maintain his intellectual integrity, a person chooses to base his life in the factual or cognitive realm, he cuts himself off—both in theory and in practice—from those values inherent in the valuational realm. If, on the other hand, a person chooses to maintain his "humanity" by basing his life in the valuational or non-cognitive realm, he has difficulty appreciating the values inherent in the factual realm.

Thus the dichotomy under consideration is as unfortunate as it is widespread. The only way to avoid its consequences is to construct an interpretation of experience and knowledge which is founded upon a more holistic base.

Part Two

THE SOLUTION:
THE CASE FOR TACIT KNOWLEDGE

IV: A Point of Departure: Language as Functional

It is one thing to point out and decry the existence of an epistemological dualism; it is quite another to supply a more adequate theory of knowledge. Nevertheless, my main effort in this part will be to do precisely that. Such a task must, of course, be approached with a great deal of circumspection and a spirit of approximation. Obviously, the profundity and thoroughness of Kant's scholarship will not be duplicated to any degree. On the other hand, Kant's dichotomies must be replaced, and I do believe that the following chapters reflect the important features which such a replacement must have.

Where to begin? Where does one look for a point of departure from which to construct a fresh and more adequate understanding of knowledge? To be more specific, where does one look for an epistemological foundation which will provide for the possibility of religious knowledge? In my own wrestling with this problem I have made the most headway by approaching it on the basis of the insights provided by what is termed "linguistic analysis" or "ordinary language" philosophy. In particular, I have been strongly influenced by the later writings of Ludwig Wittgenstein and J. L. Austin, and it is to their work that I will look in this chapter for an initial clue to the solution of the problem set out in Part One.

The conviction underlying this chapter is that the best way to obtain an understanding of the major features of reality and experience is to pay close attention to the function and structure of language. Without attempting to decide the question of the problematic relation between language and reality, it is obvious that the two are very closely related. It is my contention that the structure of reality is mediated through experience, and that experience itself is mediated through language. Thus the main characteristics of both reality and experience are reflected in the various uses and functions of language.

Substantial progress in investigating the possibility of religious knowledge can be made by taking a close look at the actual language of and about religious experience. Although a more detailed account of "God-talk" will be given in a later chapter, it is of value to raise the issue briefly now in order to keep the central concern of the book in focus. The effect of the epistemological dichotomies under attack upon the problem of the knowledge of God has been disastrous indeed. This claim could hardly be stated more pointedly and relevantly than Michael Novak does in the following quotation. Herein lies the real value in beginning the reconstruction of religious epistemology by considering the nature and function of language.

> There is a special temptation for Christians living after the Enlightenment to try to spell out by their experience in the language of the Enlightenment. To succumb to that temptation is to invite failure. From the time of Descartes onward (Pascal said he would never forgive Descartes for speaking of God in this language) a special class of interpretations has surrounded the word "reason," such that anyone who begins to use the language of intelligence according to that class of interpretations must end by placing "reason" and "faith" on opposite sides of a divide. There are many things about belief in God that cannot be said in words dear to the Enlightenment. There are many experiences of human life which are spoken of only with great difficulty, if at all, in the systems clustering around the various canons of "reason" employed by post-Cartesian philosophers. To every age of philosophers some debt is owed; but each age also has its deficiencies. One deficiency not yet met by philosophers is the lack of a suitable language for talking about intelligent subjectivity.[1]

1. THE PICTURE THEORY OF MEANING

It is difficult to overestimate the pervasive and insidious nature of what might be called the "commonsense" view of language. This commonsense view sees language as composed of words which *name* objects, or qualities of objects, and statements which *represent* the relationships among these objects and/or qualities. On the popular level this view of language is exceedingly common, and thus it is given as an explanation both of the way children learn their mother tongue and of the way adults acquire a second language. On a semi-sophisticated level this view is often expressed in the writings of "general semanticists," such as S. I. Hayakawa.[2] Here the dominant model for understanding language is that of a map. Language is seen as an attempt to represent or picture reality in a one-to-one correspondence. Or one might cite the example of a prominent interpreter of scientific developments who, when discussing the relationship between language and computers, says:

> We express our thoughts in words. For this reason, the structure of thought is paralleled by the structure of language. . . . We must distinguish between two kinds of sentences. Some sentences . . . have a clear meaning. Other sentences have *no* meaning. . . . A statement that has meaning is called a *proposition*. Every proposition is either true or false.[3]

This interpretation of language has a long tradition on the philosophical level as well as the popular. However, there is a sense in which its presence on the philosophical level has been more tacit than explicit. Plato seems to imply such an interpretation when he insists that abstract nouns must stand for, or refer to, something which transcends empirical experience. In modern thought both the continental rationalists and the British empiricists consistently fell back on talk about "the objects of thought" to which our words refer. It was not until the twentieth century that philosophers began to focus their attention on what might be termed "the philosophy of language." It is with this focus that the following pages will be concerned.

The "picture theory of meaning," as it has come to be called, received a highly sophisticated presentation early in this century in the writings of Bertrand Russell[4] and the young Ludwig Wittgenstein.[5] The heart of this theory is the belief that reality is composed of all possible *facts*, or states of affairs, and that the world is made up of those possible facts which have been actualized. Facts are neither objects nor qualities but are relations among objects and qualities; for example, it is a fact that grass is green, and it is a fact that the furniture in this room is standing on the floor. It is usually implied by the holders of this theory that this account of reality in terms of facts is comprehensive enough to treat adequately the whole range of human experience. Thus the fact that John loves Mary can also be understood as a relationship between two objects, John and Mary. Whether such an account is adequate will have to be pursued a bit later. "The world is all that is the case. The world is the totality of facts, not of things."[6]

Given this view of reality and experience, the proponents of the picture theory of language go on to maintain that language is to be understood as a collection of propositions which picture possible facts, or reality. The basic components of propositions are words, which serve as names of objects and qualities. "A name means an object. The object is its meaning. . . . In a proposition a name is the representative of an object."[7] The relationship which the proposition pictures is not represented by names, but by the logical relationship of the names in the proposition. Of course, some propositions picture more than one fact, but nevertheless their purpose is to mirror the same logical relationships as the states of affairs about which they speak. Thus it is that according to this view meaning is a function of the pictorial relation between propositions and facts. A statement is said to be meaningful if it pictures a possible fact and meaningless if it does not. As Wittgenstein puts it:

> One name stands for one thing, another for another thing, and
> they are combined with one another. In this way the whole
> group—like a *tableau vivant*—presents a state of affairs.
>   The possibility of propositions is based on the principle that
> objects have signs as their representatives.[8]

Furthermore a meaningful statement is true if it pictures
actual facts and false if it only pictures possible ones. Thus
truth is a function of the correspondence between propositions and states of affairs. To quote Wittgenstein again:

> What a picture represents is its sense. The agreement or dis-
> agreement of its sense with reality constitutes its truth or fal-
> sity. In order to tell whether a picture is true or false we must
> compare it with reality.[9]

It is a much debated question whether the picture theory of meaning makes it necessary to ground all meaningful propositions in sensory observation and all true
propositions in empirical verification.[10] It is true, however, that the theory does lend itself to such an interpretation, as will become clear in the remaining remarks of
this section.

It was upon the foundation laid by the picture theory of
meaning that the movement which was first called "logical
positivism," and later "logical empiricism," took its rise.
The group of scientifically-minded philosophers known as
"The Vienna Circle"[11] sought to combine the insights of
Russell and Wittgenstein with those of scientific methodology in order to free philosophy from its traditional
quagmire of pseudo-problems. Hans Reichenbach, who was
discussed briefly in Chapter One, represents the concerns
of this group quite forcefully. The clearest and most influential exposition of this position in the English language
was given by A. J. Ayer in his *Language, Truth and Logic*.

The essentials of logical empiricism were sketched out in
the first chapter, and will only be summarized at this
juncture. The reason for such a summary is to indicate the
logical connection between the picture theory of meaning
and the contemporary situation in philosophy. The point

to be stressed about logical empiricism is its insistence that the possibility of empirical verification be used as the criterion for determining the meaningfulness of a given statement. If it is possible to empirically confirm or disconfirm a statement, then it has meaning, even if it happens to be false. To put the point in the terms of the picture theory: the way to tell whether or not a statement pictures a possible state of affairs is to determine whether or not it can be "compared" with reality. If it can, then it is meaningful, and if it cannot, then it is not meaningful.

There is, to be sure, a separate criterion for determining the meaningfulness of the statements of formal logic and mathematics. This was true with Russell and Wittgenstein as well. However, this aspect of logical empiricism need not be considered in this discussion because, in spite of its rather technical nature, it does not alter the major points being presented.

On the basis of this criterion of meaning, the logical empiricists have gone on to eliminate metaphysics, theology, and ethics from the realm of meaningful discourse. Here again appears the rigid dichotomy between the domains of fact and value which was the theme of Part One. This is the real point of connection between the problem of the fact-value split which plagues contemporary thought and the picture theory of meaning upon which it is based. Any attempt to overcome the dichotomy between cognitivity and non-cognitivity must come to grips with the picture theory of meaning. Before turning to this task, however, we must make two additional points about the connection between the picture theory of meaning and the problem of fact and value.

First, it should be understood that the picture theory of meaning is implicit in the fact-value dichotomy of Immanuel Kant. Although the terminology of logical empiricism was not available to Kant, and although he does not address himself directly to the problem of language, Kant's philosophy does necessarily imply a view of language essentially similar to the picture theory. As Michael Novak makes clear in the statement quoted earlier, the language of early modern philosophy "stacks the deck" in favor of seeing language as a process of applying names to objects.

The very basis of Kant's distinction between the phenomena of cognitive experience and the noumena of unexperienced, or ultimate, reality lies in a view of cognitive experience as representational in nature. The objects of thought are conceived of as representations of the objects of reality. Thus concepts and conceptual language are to be viewed as representational in nature. Kant's writings are replete with statements and arguments relying upon such a view of thought and language. The following quotation will suffice as an illustration:

> The capacity (receptivity) for receiving representations through the mode in which we are affected by objects, is entitled *sensibility*. Objects are *given* to us by means of sensibility, and it alone yields us *intuitions*; they are *thought* through the understanding, and from the understanding arise *concepts*. But all thought must, directly or indirectly, by way of certain characters, relate ultimately to intuitions, and therefore, with us, to sensibility, because in no other way can an object be given to us.[12]

Secondly, it undoubtedly has not gone unnoticed that thus far nothing has been said about the relationship of existentialism to the picture theory of language. The main point that needs to be made in this regard is that although existentialist thinkers often seem to be aware of the limitations of the representational view of thought and language, they rarely offer a viable replacement for it. In fact, the most common existentialist move is to reject all forms of direct, or object-centered, talk as a tool of objectifying and dehumanizing positivism. This tendency is clearly exemplified in the discussion of Heidegger, Kierkegaard and Bultmann in Chapter One. The attempt to identify value-centered talk with poetry or religious myth represents yet another expression of the fact-value dichotomy upon which both empiricism and existentialism are based.

Furthermore, the fact that the picture theory of language is rejected by the existentialists, without any attempt to replace it with a more comprehensive and sophisticated theory, forces them into the position of either embracing poetic mysticism and silence, or unconsciously falling back on the picture theory itself. One can find frequent examples of both fates, each as unsatisfactory as the other. What is needed is a view of language that will do justice to the insights of both empiricism and existentialism without separating them—and thus separating human nature—into two air-tight compartments. Fortunately, the foundation for such a theory of language has been laid in the later works of Wittgenstein and J. L. Austin.

2. LANGUAGE AND MEANING

"What can be said at all can be said clearly, and what we cannot talk about we must consign to silence."[13] In these words the younger Wittgenstein summed up the major thesis of his earlier work. These words clearly reflect the dichotomy against which Wittgenstein's later philosophy is directed. The dominant theme of Wittgenstein's later thought is that language is a multi-functional, "many splendored" phenomenon which cannot be limited to the confines of logic and science. The major shortcoming of his earlier view of language was its total reliance upon the picture theory of language and meaning. Although in his later works he readily acknowledged that language is sometimes employed to name objects and picture states of affairs, Wittgenstein insisted that to hold this function as paradigmatic of all of language inevitably leads to the exclusion of many other uses of language from the realm of meaningful discourse. "A main cause of philosophical disease—a one-sided diet: one nourishes one's thinking with only one kind of example."[14]

Thus the major liability of the picture theory of meaning is that it fails to take into account the many uses of language other than naming objects and representing facts.

Instead of maintaining that there are essentially only two kinds of sentences (cognitive and non-cognitive), philosophers ought to be able to see that there are countless uses of language which do not fit into the neat categories implied by the picture theory. Who is to say which of the following uses of language, offered by Wittgenstein, are cognitive and which are non-cognitive, which are factual and which are valuational?

> Review the multiplicity of language-games in the following examples, and in others:
>> Giving orders, and obeying them—
>> Describing the appearance of an object, or giving its measurements—
>> Constructing an object from a description (a drawing)—
>> Reporting an event—
>> Speculating about an event—
>> Forming and testing a hypothesis—
>> Presenting the results of an experiement in tables and diagrams—
>> Making up a story; and reading it—
>> Play-acting—
>> Singing catches—
>> Guessing riddles—
>> Making a joke, telling it—
>> Solving a problem in practical arithmetic—
>> Translating from one language into another—
>> Asking, thanking, cursing, greeting, praying.[15]

A bit later in the *Philosophical Investigations* Wittgenstein addresses himself more directly to the "naming" aspect of the picture theory by denying that talking about objects is all that is done with language:

> . . .in fact we do the most various things with our sentences. Think of exclamations alone, with their completely different functions. Water! Away! Ow! Help! Fine! No! Are you still inclined to call these words "names of objects"?[16]

There are three main themes in Wittgenstein's later philosophy which go together to form the basis of a whole new understanding of language, and ultimately of experience itself. During the discussion of these three dimensions it must be borne in mind that they provide the where-withal for undermining the fact-value dichotomy by dis-mantling the picture theory of meaning upon which it is based. My contention is that Wittgenstein's later thought provides a major clue to constructing an interpretation of experience and knowledge which is far superior to that underlying the contemporary epistemological stalemate. Hopefully, this more adequate interpretation can serve as the basis for reopening the question of the possibility of religious knowledge.

The first major theme of Wittgenstein's fresh approach is that language must be understood as a human instru-ment, or tool, for the accomplishment of various and diverse tasks. Viewing language this way has, of course, several important implications. To begin, this approach calls attention to the fact that statements do not exist and have meaning in a vacuum, but have meaning because they are made by persons seeking to fulfill certain purposes. This fact renders inappropriate the logical empiricist attempt to classify all statements as either factual or valu-ational irrespective of why, where, and by whom the statements are made. Thus Wittgenstein's remark: "One cannot guess how a word functions. One has to *look at* its use and learn from that."[17] Meaning, then, must be under-stood as a function of use, not solely as a function of representation. Statements have different uses and thus different meanings. Even the same set of words, or sen-tence, may have a variety of meanings, depending upon how it is used.

Two examples of the same set of words having a variety of uses and thus meanings, will have to suffice. Consider the following sentence from J. L. Austin: "The bull is about to charge." This set of words can be said to have, among others, the following, rather obvious, meanings: It can function as 1) a description, 2) a warning, 3) an example of English grammar, 4) a joke, 5) a signal, 6) a coded message, 7) an example of the multi-functional nature of language (as is the case now), 8) a translation of a non-English utterance, 9) as esthetic evaluation, etc. It clearly makes little sense to insist on being given the "meaning" of this or any set of words apart from an awareness of the context within which it is uttered. Or again, take the slang phrases which employ the term "out" in one way or another. When something is "out" it is taken to be bad or passé—as opposed to "in," which connotes value or stylishness. Yet, when something is "way out" it is taken to be especially good or stylish, and functions as a synonym for "in." Such subtle distinctions in meaning can be grasped only by paying close attention to usage.

Wittgenstein brings out the variety of uses and meanings in language by comparing words and statements to tools in a toolbox, or to pieces in a chess game.[18] In each case the "meaning" of these individual instruments can be established only by determining their function, or how they are used.

> It is like looking into the cabin of a locomotive. We see handles all looking more or less alike. (Naturally, since they are all supposed to be handled.) But one is the handle of a crank which can be moved continuously (it regulates the opening of a valve); another is the handle of a switch, which has only two effective positions, it is either off or on; a third is the handle of a brake-lever, the harder one pulls on it, the harder it brakes; a fourth, the handle of a pump: it has an effect only so long as it is moved to and fro.[19]

Meaning, then, is not something which "stands behind" language, nor that at which language points, nor even the mental "objects of understanding." The meaning of a given statement is the reason why and the way in which it is made. Perhaps it would be best not to speak at all of what statements mean, and simply speak of what persons mean in their use of statements.

It should be mentioned that armed with this conception of language and meaning, Wittgenstein proceeds to do battle not only with his own former views on philosophy and language, but with other specific philosophical views as well. Although to trace out his wrestling with these problems would constitute a digression from the main stream of thought in this chapter, it should be noted that Wittgenstein severely criticized the traditional interpretations of talk about pain, understanding, and the relation between the mind and the body. In each case he takes an anti-dualistic stance toward these subjects, and I will return to some of his specific arguments in later chapters.[20]

Wittgenstein summarizes his main objection to the narrow rigidity of the picture theory in a statement which seems aimed directly at his summary of the *Tractatus*, as quoted at the beginning of this section.

> The more narrowly we examine actual language, the sharper becomes the conflict between it and our requirement. (For the crystal-line purity of logic was, of course, not a *result of investigation*: it was a requirement). The conflict becomes intolerable; the requirement is now in danger of becoming empty.—We have got on to slippery ice where there is no friction and so in a certain sense the conditions are ideal, but also, just because of that, we are unable to walk. We want to walk: so we need *friction*. Back to the rough ground![21]

For those who want to communicate by their use of language, the rough-and-ready texture of ordinary language, though lacking logical purity, is absolutely necessary.

The second major theme in Wittgenstein's fresh approach to language is his concept of "language-games." Given that the meaning of statements is to be grasped by ascertaining their use, it is equally important to be able to fit a given contextual utterance into the broader background of a particular aspect of human behavior. Wittgenstein used the term "language-game" to call attention to the fact that speaking is an activity having significance only against the backdrop of certain human endeavors and the participation of other persons. Statements are invested with meaning by persons who speak not only in specific contexts, but also within the various dimensions of human activity. Thus meaning is determined by the rules of the various, overlapping language-games which together comprise a given language. Each language-game—"giving orders, and obeying them, describing the appearance of an object, or giving its measurements," etc.—could be viewed as a region, or neighborhood, within the overall language. To some extent, each region of language develops independently of the others, but there are also many overlappings and exchanges among the various regions.

Aside from the obvious point that Wittgenstein's use of the term "game" must not be construed as an attempt to demean language, there are several other points about his concept of language-games which bear mentioning. One is that once the various functions of language are seen in this light, the claim that any one function, or language-game, has priority over the others is seen to be quite silly. Here again Wittgenstein's position serves to undercut both the scientific bias of empiricism and the ethico-religious bias of existentialism. Not only is no region of language more or less important than any other, but the lines of demarcation between the regions are not hard and fast. Thus the appropriateness, or lack of it, of any move in language depends upon its function.

> To say "This combination of words makes no sense" excludes it from the sphere of language and thereby bounds the domain of language. But when one draws a boundary it may be for various kinds of reason. If I surround an area with a fence or a line or otherwise, the purpose may be to prevent someone from getting in or out; but it may also be part of a game and the players be supposed, say to jump over the boundary; or it may shew where the property of one man ends and that of another begins; and so on. So if I draw a boundary line that is not yet to say what I am drawing it for.[22]

Another point inherent in the concept of language-games is that the rules for such games are not, and need not be, explicitly nor precisely stated. "When I give the description: 'The ground was quite covered with plants'—do you want to say that I don't know what I am talking about until I can give a definition of a plant?"[23] The point here is that using language is not something in which we begin with precise definitions and proceed with rigid rules. In this sense, too, it is like learning to play a game, since one usually begins learning a game by simply imitating what the other players do. How many people who know how to play bridge or basketball quite well have ever read a rulebook? The implied assumption of the picture theory of meaning, that language is composed of names of objects which can be combined in certain ways according to statable rules, simply does not jibe with the facts. Language is a highly complex and constantly changing phenomenon, and therein lies its overall strength and effectiveness. Moreover, learning how to use language is largely a tacit process involving far more than learning simple rules. One shows that he understands the meaning of various statements and language-games not by citing definitions and rules, but by participating successfully in the give and take of everyday discourse.[24]

The third major theme in Wittgenstein's interpretation of language is his concept of "forms of life." Just as specific statements have meaning only in concrete contexts, and these contexts have meaning only as part of a larger language-game, so language-games themselves have meaning only within the broader framework of the full range of human life. "Here the term 'language-*game*' is meant to bring into prominence the fact that the *speaking* of language is part of an activity, or of a form of life."[25] Wittgenstein does not say enough about this concept to allow an interpreter to be very explicit about what he had in mind. Nevertheless, it is quite clear that he meant to stress the point that far from being something that persons do in addition to living, using language is an integral part of the business of being human.

The phrase "form of life" occurs most frequently in Wittgenstein's writings in connection with the question of the justification of a particular language-game. "What has to be accepted, the given, is—so one could say—forms of life."[26] With respect to this question of the justification of a broad pattern of linguistic behavior, Wittgenstein makes the following comment, which dovetails with his notion of forms of life:

> "How am I able to obey a rule?"—if this is not a question about causes, then it is about the justification for my following the rule in the way I do.
> If I have exhausted the justifications I have reached bedrock, and my spade is turned. Then I am inclined to say: "This is simply what I do."[27]

Such a way of putting the matter suggests that in the final analysis language-games may well be arbitrary conventions, devoid of any real justification. Without entering into the deep and interesting philosophical issue about the relation of Wittgenstein's thought to "linguistic conventionalism," let me just say that I do not think that he took linguistic uses and activities to have arbitrary bases.[28] Although language is a human and social production that grows and changes with the change of conditions, it is also part of the very fabric of human existence. There is strong anthropological and psychological evidence to support the position that language and humanity are logically coextensive.[29] It is in this sense that Wittgenstein's following remarks are to be understood:

> "So you are saying that human agreement decides what is true and what is false?—It is what human beings *say* that is true and false; and they agree in the *language* they use. That is not agreement in opinions but in form of life.
> If language is to be a means of communication there must be agreement not only in definitions but also (queer as this may sound) in judgments. This seems to abolish logic, but does not do so.—It is one thing to describe methods of measurement, and another to obtain and state results of measurement. But what we call "measuring" is partly determined by a certain constancy in results of measurement.[30]

By way of summary, I will now set out what, for the purpose of this chapter, are the most salient conclusions implied by Wittgenstein's revolutionary theory of language. It will be recalled that the purpose of this chapter is to explore the later thought of Wittgenstein and J. L. Austin in order to uncover clues to a view of experience and knowledge that will overcome the dichotomized nature of modern epistemology.

First, it can hardly be denied that the main themes of Wittgenstein's conception of language insist upon the necessity of maintaining a great deal of tolerance toward the various uses and developments of language. This *principle of tolerance* is one of the most valuable contributions made by Wittgenstein and "ordinary language philosophy." It completely, and convincingly, contravenes the narrowness of the picture theory of language underlying much of the fact-value dichotomy. A vast number of our meaningful uses of language do not fit into the pre-established molds prescribed by the picture theory. In fact, there are a variety of uses which are meaningful even though their logic seems to defy classification altogether.[31] These uses have been the special study of one of Wittgenstein's foremost "disciples," John Wisdom. In formulating the thesis which underlies his study of seemingly odd, or paradoxical uses, Wisdom states that

> ...questions which neither further observation and experience nor yet further thought will settle may yet present real problems and even problems as to matters of fact. It is submitted that questions which "have no answers" may yet present problems which have solutions, that questions which "have no answers" can and, mostly, do evince some inadequacy in our apprehension of things, and that when this inadequacy is removed by thought, which while it is helped by precedent is not bound by it, we gain a new view of what is possible and sometimes of what is actual.[32]

The first clue to the construction of a sound view of knowledge, then, is this: Such a view can ill afford to begin by segregating the various uses of language into hermetically sealed compartments. A second salient conclusion following from Wittgenstein's fresh approach is that language, far from being a distinct and autonomous entity standing between persons and reality, is actually the medium in which both personhood and reality can be said to exist. In a sense, language must now be viewed as an *extension of both selfhood and reality*. That language is an extension of the self can be seen from the fact that no lines of demarcation can be drawn between one's self, one's form of life, and one's various uses of language. This point is emphasized by Wittgenstein's conception of language as a tool or instrument for human use. Tools are often best understood as extensions of those who use them, especially when the user is an expert. As both the common expression and our entire social culture make clear, "A man is his word." Likewise, it is impossible to draw lines of demarcation between language and reality. In a definite sense reality is so mediated by means of language that the two become indistinguishable upon close analysis.

This conclusion clearly militates against both the picture theory of logical empiricism and the basic dichotomies of Kant's philosophy. Both of these approaches proceed as if it were not only possible, but relatively easy, to distinguish these aspects of human experience from one another. They both fall back on a representational dualism in thought and language which simply cannot be established and which leads to more difficulties than it solves. Here then is another clue to a more adequate approach to experience and knowledge: The relationships between the self, thought, language, and reality must be conceived of as continuous and holistic in nature.

The final clue I will mention as inherent in Wittgenstein's thought pertains to the nature of meaning itself. On the basis of the concepts of use and language-games, it can be concluded that *meaning is a "logically primitive" notion*. There are several facets to this phrase, borrowed from P. F. Strawson,[33] which bear investigation. First, the phrase is meant to indicate that the concept and/or the term "meaning" is "beneath," or not subject to, definition. Thus it can be thought of as undefinable, or logically simple. Nevertheless, the concept is not without meaning, as is made perfectly clear by its obvious usefulness, even in this present sentence. One does not have to define "meaning" or the act of pointing before teaching another person to use language. Second, in saying that meaning is a logically primitive notion, I am trying to call attention to the fact that meaning is something that is grasped "tacitly," or indirectly, not explicitly. It is this ability to grasp meaning, or the significance of symbolization, which initiates the process of becoming a person and enables one to enter into that form of life known as humanity. Indeed, it is impossible to say what "meaning" means until one has already grasped what "means" means; and then it is no longer necessary!

The significance of this clue for the task of this second part of the book is hard to overemphasize. To view meaning as logically primitive is to deny the legitimacy of any view of language which implies that meaning resides in the logical structure of a given sentence. The representational theory of thought and language which underlies the fact-value dichotomy is found wanting on precisely this point. Meaning is not a function of logic and explicit definition, but of use and tacit awareness. Therefore it need not be restricted to the so-called "factual realm," but can be seen to be active in a variety of language uses.

3. LANGUAGE AND TRUTH

Having summed up the insights of the later Wittgenstein, together with their implications for the task of constructing a view of knowledge that overcomes the dualism of modern epistemology, I turn now to a parallel treatment of the thought of J. L. Austin. Although he rarely, if ever, openly acknowledges any debt to the work of Wittgenstein, it is obvious to even the casual reader that Austin draws heavily upon Wittgenstein's main themes.

Austin is credited in philosophical circles with having "discovered" what he termed the "performative" function of language. By this term Austin put the spotlight on certain uses of language which seek, not to *describe* some state of affairs, but to *perform* an act. He was convinced that for too long philosophers had paid attention only to the descriptive, or constative, function of language, assuming that all language had description as its goal. Austin called this assumption "the descriptive fallacy," and the goal of his early work was to establish the equal legitimacy of the performative use of language. This performative function involves the use of certain conventional phrases, said in fairly well prescribed circumstances, by means of which an act beyond the act of making a statement is accomplished.

As Austin put it:

> Suppose, for example, that in the course of a marriage cere-mony I say, as people will, "I do"—(sc. take this woman to be my lawful wedded wife). Or again, suppose that I tread on your toe and say "I apologize." Or again, suppose that I have the bottle of champagne in my hand and say "I name this ship the Queen Elizabeth." Or suppose I say "I bet you sixpence it will rain tomorrow." In all these cases it would be absurd to regard the thing that I say as a report of the performance of the action which is undoubtedly done—the action of betting, or christening, or apologizing. We should say rather that, in saying what I do, I actually perform that action. When I say "I name this ship the Queen Elizabeth" I do not describe the christening ceremony, I actually perform the christening; and when I say "I do" (sc. take this woman to be my lawful wedded wife), I am not reporting on a marriage, I am indulging in it.[34]

Even while he worked at calling attention to performa-tive utterances, Austin was aware that no hard and fast line could be drawn between them and descriptive, or cogni-tive, utterances.[35] Yet, the more he worked at pinpointing the defining characteristics which allow one, if only in a rough and ready way, to distinguish performative from descriptive utterances, Austin became increasingly con-vinced that such a pinpointing was ill-conceived. In his later work, then, Austin concludes that the reason this task could not succeed was that it had been predicated on the assumption that statements can have only one function at a time.[36] The main thesis of the final phase of Austin's work is that all speech is best understood as an activity which consists of a variety of "forces," all obtaining simultaneously. He cites three main kinds of speech-acts: 1) the saying of certain words (*what* is said), which is termed the "locutionary act"; 2) the purpose of saying the certain words (*why* it is said), which is termed the "illocutionary act"; 3) the results of saying the certain words (*effects*), which is termed the "perlocutionary act."[37]

Austin is especially interested in the distinction between locutionary force and illocutionary acts. He seems to have begun, at least, by associating "meaning" with the former and "force" with the latter. Although this is not the place to enter into a critical analysis of the fine points of Austin's theories, I will say that it is more consistent with the thrust of his original insights in these matters to interpret locution, illocution, and perlocution as simultaneous forces of a given speech-act, rather than as separate acts within a larger act.[38] Moreover, this interpretation would open the door to associating "meaning" with each force, or with the three combined, rather than just with the locutionary force. I am convinced that this interpretation is more in line with Austin's main concern, as the following considerations will make clear.

In much the same way that he had become disillusioned about finding a definite line of demarcation between constatives and performatives, Austin concludes that the illocutionary as well as the locutionary forces of a statement are subject to evaluation in terms of their appropriateness. While there has been a tendency to associate "true" and "false" exclusively with the latter, this should not blur the fact that the former can also be accepted or rejected on the basis of criteria which are nonetheless real for being less explicit. As Austin puts it:

> Can we be sure that stating truly is a different *class* of assessment from arguing soundly, advising well, judging fairly, and blaming justifiably? Do these not have something to do in complicated ways with facts? The same is true also of exercitives such as naming, appointing, bequeathing, and betting.

> Facts come in as well as our knowledge or opinion about facts.[39]

In addition, the question of the relation of truth and falsity to the various forces of a speech-act can be applied to the "cognitive purity" of so-called factual judgments, or constative statements. Austin raises and answers the question in the following fashion: "In real life, as opposed to the simple situations envisaged in logical theory, one cannot always answer in a simple manner whether it is true or false."[40] Austin substantiates his answer by offering as an example the statement, "France is hexagonal." He maintains that the proper classification of this description is neither "true" nor "false," but "rough"!

After thus rejecting a strict true-false dichotomy, one fetish of logical empiricism, Austin goes on to challenge another important fetish, namely the dichotomy between judgments of fact and judgments of value. He begins by sorting out a good number of kinds of utterances in which factual and valuational concerns are to varying degrees blended. His general conclusion is that a large variety of the kinds of judgments which must be, and are, uttered in everyday life simply render a rigid distinction between fact and value unhelpful. In one place Austin illustrates this claim by referring to the obvious blending of the two types of judgments in the verdict of an umpire.[41]

By means of the following "morals," Austin summarizes his overall position:

> (A) The total speech act in the total speech situation is the *only actual* phenomenon which, in the last resort, we are engaged in elucidating.
> (B) Stating, describing, &c., are *just two* names among a very great many others for illocutionary acts; they have no unique position.
> (C) In particular, they have no unique position over the matter of being true or false, because truth and falsity are (except by an artificial abstraction which is always possible and legitimate for certain purposes) not names for relations, qualities, or what not, but for a dimension of assessment—how

the words stand in respect of satisfactoriness to the facts, events, situations, &c., to which they refer.

(D) By the same token, the familiar contrast of "normative or evaluative" as opposed to the factual is in need, like so many dichotomies, of elimination.

(E) We may well suspect that the theory of "meaning" as equivalent to "sense and reference" will certainly require some weeding-out and reformulating in terms of the distinction between locutionary and illocutionary acts.[42]

Before bringing this chapter to a close, it will be helpful to draw attention to the major clues which can be garnered from Austin's work for the construction of a fresh approach to the understanding of experience and knowledge in general, and to the possibility of religious knowledge in particular. I will focus on those clues which are not repetitious of those drawn from Wittgenstein's work.

My first point pertains to the general thrust of Austin's work, as it is revealed in the title of his book *How To Do Things With Words*. It should be obvious by now that his approach to the relationship between language and action is diametrically opposed to that implied by the more traditional interpretation of language. As we have seen, the more traditional interpretation views language as a distinct entity, existing between persons and reality in such a way as to keep them logically separate from one another. Austin's interpretation, however, views language as a means by which the speaker projects himself into reality and thereby changes it. The traditional view dichotomizes language (thought) and action (reality), whereas Austin's view blends them in a functional manner. Speaking is, after all, an action through which the gap between the self and reality is spanned.

At the same time, it should not go unnoticed that Austin's emphasis on language as an activity is a two-way street. Not only can one *do* things *with* words, but one can also *say* things *without* words. That is, once the self, thought, language, action, and reality are conceived as points on a continuum, rather than as totally distinct ontological entities, the way is open to acknowledge the obvious fact that verbal symbolization is not the only means of speaking. In fact, a strong case can be made for the position that most communication between persons is accomplished by means other than the spoken or written word. These other means include not only such obvious, yet important, factors as voice tone, facial expression, and bodily gestures, but they include conventional and non-conventional actions as well. When the football referee throws down his white flag and places his hands on his hips, even the nominal fan knows that an "offside" is being indicated. Moreover, when a husband buries his face deeper into the evening paper (or does any number of non-conventional acts), his wife gets the message that there will be no new hat this Easter. Even silence, in the right circumstances, speaks loudly.

The implications of this new understanding of the relation between language and action for a fresh start in epistemology are great. Austin has made a convincing case for viewing language as a flexible, open-ended phenomenon with no hard and fast lines drawn between it and the speaker on the one hand, and between it and the surrounding world on the other. This view of language disposes of the necessity of confining meaning to a narrowly prescribed class of statements. With a broader and enriched understanding of language and meaning, it is possible to avoid the dualistic stalemate inherent in these interpretations, be they existentialist or empiricist, that are based on a dichotomized view of human existence.

A second major conclusion which can be derived from Austin's thought is that *all uses of language are multidimensional in nature*. His insight into the various "forces" of a speech-act makes it quite clear that the more standard—and stalemate-producing—distinctions between cognitive and non-cognitive judgments will not hold up. Whenever a statement is made it has cognitive and non-cognitive force simultaneously. Thus it is not helpful to speak of factual and valuational judgments as mutually exclusive, but it is helpful to speak of the factual and valuational dimensions of a given judgment. There are numerous examples in Austin's writings of statements that illustrate this multi-dimensional nature of judgments, but perhaps a brief extension of the topic will contribute to a fuller understanding of its significance.

Take the statement "The Beatles write good music." A value judgment such as this is usually classified as non-cognitive because it does not "picture" any factual situation, but only expresses an individual value judgment. Now to begin with, this statement is dependent upon the factual dimension of experience for its meaning in the sense that it implies that there exists a musical group known as The Beatles. Furthermore, that this statement is not devoid of cognitive meaning is clearly shown by the fact that it is appropriate to ask the person who utters it his reasons for saying such a thing; and if he has uttered it sincerely, he will be able to give reasons for believing it to be the case. Although the reasons that he gives will not necessarily convince his questioner, this does not detract from the cognitivity of the original statement. A claim has been made which implies a certain state of affairs and about which it is reasonable to argue.

By thus broadening the concept of cognitivity one discovers yet another clue to the development of an epistemological foundation which cuts through the impasse confronting contemporary philosophical and theological thought. This broader and more flexible understanding of cognitivity in language points to the possibility of viewing experience as multi-dimensional, and of thereby formulating a broader and more flexible interpretation of knowledge and truth. This, in turn, may open up the possibility of religious knowledge and truth.

Finally, there is one other conclusion I would like to draw from Austin's work. In a way this conclusion is simply the other side of the one I have just discussed. This time, take the statement, "The Beatles write music." Here, under standard interpretation, is a cognitive, or factual, judgment which is free of valuational implications. Yet such questions as "Is what they write to be called 'music'?" clearly raise some valuational difficulties about the "cognitive purity" of the statement. Further, it remains the case that someone must make the statement before it is a real statement, and when someone does it always takes on a valuational dimension in the sense that the speaker is giving his "personal backing" to the statement. Thus *truth is a function of personal commitment*. There is a sense in which every statement must necessarily participate in both the factual and valuational dimensions simultaneously. Technically speaking, each statement should be prefaced by the phrase, "I say," thereby indicating the speaker's responsibility for making it. Although it might appear that such a prefacing of all statements with "I say" would be superfluous, it can hardly be considered so if it serves as a reminder that statement-making involves personal commitment.[43]

Another way to make this point is by maintaining that Austin's work stands as a direct challenge to the logical empiricist bias against the possibility of metaphorical language's being cognitively true. This bias was documented in Paul Edwards' thought in Chapter One. Austin's insights challenge this point of view in that they render it impossible to restrict the concept of cognitive truth to the domain of factual assertions. When one begins to explore the vast variety of locutions which in varying degrees participate in the cognitive dimension it becomes clear that the so-called "emotive" or "valuational" uses of language, such as the metaphorical, can be shown to function cognitively. Here again the fact-value dichotomy comes up wanting.

Max Black, whose thought has been influenced by both Wittgenstein and Austin, has addressed himself explicitly to the question of the cognitive status of metaphorical language. He objects strongly and cogently to the assumption that one can always translate whatever is of cognitive value (an interesting locution!) in a metaphor into the "plain language" of empirical assertion:

> One of the points I most wish to stress is that the loss in such cases is a loss in cognitive content; the relevant weakness of the literal paraphrase is not that it may be tiresomely prolix or boringly explicit (or deficient in qualities of style); it fails to be a translation because it fails to give the insight that the metaphor did.[44]

The long-range significance of this fresh view of the relation between language, commitment, and truth for the mapping-out of a non-dualistic epistemology should be quite obvious. If empirical assertions can no longer be said to have a monopoly on the cognitive function of language, it can hardly be maintained that knowledge is limited to the logical and empirical dimension of experience. Thus another clue has been provided to the formulation of an epistemology which can encompass the insights of both empiricism and existentialism.

The purpose of this chapter has been to examine the contributions of Wittgenstein and Austin with an eye to finding clues toward solving the problem of dualism presented in Part One. With these insights in mind, I now turn to a more straightforward attempt at constructing such a solution.

V: Knowledge as Awareness: Dimensions and Contexts

It is my conviction that the clues provided by linguistic philosophy focus themselves most clearly in terms of two main concepts: awareness and response. A sound view of language necessitates interpreting knowledge as a function of contextual, dimensional, and tacit *awareness*. Grasping meaning in language depends upon being tacitly aware of the various dimensions or forces which make up the context of any given statement. Thus knowledge is inextricably bound up with experiential awareness. In addition, a sound view of language necessitates interpreting knowledge as a function of purposeful, committed, and creative *response*. Grasping truth in language depends upon responding as a total person to experience. Thus knowledge is also inextricably bound up with integrated activity; that is, with being fully human. The unpacking of these two emphases will be the concern of this and the next chapter.

1. EXPERIENCE AS DIMENSIONAL

The model which has traditionally been used to interpret the many aspects of reality and human experience is that of different realms, or worlds. It is against this model that I wish to argue. This traditional perspective has a very ancient history. Clearly Plato, in his doctrine of the world of Forms, contributed to and built upon it. His concept of human nature as consisting of three parts (which concept

117

persisted until modern times in "faculty psychology") also played an important part in this tradition. With the advent of Christianity yet another phase of this interpretive model came into being. The New Testament writers interpreted the Christian message by means of the categories of first-century Judaism. These categories, which in large measure had been adapted from Babylonian and Persian sources, were based on the model of "other worlds," such as heaven, hell, and realms between. The fusion of the Platonic and Christian uses of this interpretive model is clearly evident throughout the history of Western thought, from Augustine to the present.

The "realm-model" of reality and experience could hardly receive a more powerful expression than it did in the philosophy of Immanuel Kant. As I have repeatedly emphasized throughout this book, Kant's dichotomies between the rational and the moral, and between the phenomenal and the noumenal, provide the basis for nearly all of modern thought. Although the realm-model is not always set forth with the rigor and absoluteness of Kant's position, it is nevertheless the dominant model for dealing with the various aspects of reality and experience.

The dilemma that the realm-model has created with respect to religious knowledge bears special treatment. To speak of God, the religious, or the spiritual as inhabiting another world, a world which by its very nature is beyond the world of human experience and knowledge, is to set up a dilemma from which modern man has been unable to extricate himself. On the one hand to claim that there is such a spiritual realm existing beyond the realm of human existence leads to insurmountable problems about how this spiritual realm is to be known. Hence the long and difficult debate about the relationship between reason and revelation. To hold out for the use of reason (natural theology) seems tantamount to denying the uniqueness of the spiritual realm, while to hold out for revelation seems to be a classic case of begging the question, since there are no criteria for distinguishing among conflicting revelational claims.

On the other horn of the dilemma, anyone who seeks to deal honestly with the challenges of the contemporary world to his religious commitment finds himself forced into talking in ways which explicitly or implicitly deny the existence of the unique, spiritual realm. This is what has happened with both the "honest to God" and "death of God" movements of the past few years. Confronted with only the two alternatives of the traditional two-storied universe and the more relevant one-storied world, the participants in these movements have been forced to opt for the second. The "God up there" versus the "God in here" dilemma is a direct result of the realm-model of experience. The way out of this dilemma is to replace the realm-model upon which it is based with one allowing for a more flexible and realistic view of reality and experience.

I should like to suggest that the model which does the best job of replacing that of realms is a model based on the concept of dimensions. Although the term "dimensions" is used often in contemporary discussions of experience, as in the writings of Paul Tillich, a closer study of the thought of those who use it almost invariably reveals that the term is being used merely as a synonym for "realm" or "world." This is especially true in Tillich's thought, as the discussion in Chapter One implies.[1] In other words, there is no particular magic in the term "dimensions." What is needed is a model based on the concept of dimensions which takes the concept seriously.

What does taking the dimension-model seriously involve? The primary point in using a dimensional approach to interpret experience is to emphasize the "simultaneity" of human existence. That is, rather than conceive of reality and experience as divided into separate realms, it is more helpful and more faithful to experience to conceive of them as having simultaneously interpenetrating dimensions. My thesis is that employing this type of model will go a long way toward overcoming the dilemmas resulting from the dichotomized view which underlies modern interpretations of both experience and language. Fact and value no longer need to be thought of as separate realms or areas, but can now be viewed as two of the more important dimensions within which man lives and acts.

It is helpful to view human experience as being comprised of four main, simultaneously interpenetrating dimensions: the physical, the moral, the personal, and the religious. The religious dimension will be spoken of more fully in a later chapter and need not be considered at this juncture.[2] By the very nature of the case, it is impossible to discuss any of these dimensions in isolation from the others. On the other hand, given the restrictions of language, it is also impossible to discuss them all simultaneously. Thus an effort must be made to speak of each one in relation to the others.

The basic relationship existing among these dimensions is one of *mediation*. That is to say, there is a definite sense in which an awareness of each of the major dimensions of human experience is mediated by an awareness of the others. One always becomes aware of one through his awareness of the rest. On the other hand, it is also true that a hierarchy exists among these dimensions. Often it is helpful to think of physical awareness as providing the base by means of which personal and moral awareness are made possible. Further, it is often helpful to think of the moral dimension as mediated through the personal dimension. Later I will argue that it is by means of all of these other dimensions that one becomes aware of the religious dimension.

The point of speaking of these dimensions as being mediated through one another is two-fold. First, the concept of mediation serves as a reminder that in no sense can the dimensions be separated from one another. The awareness of any one of them is dependent upon the awareness of the others. Second, the concept of mediation should make it clear that the awareness of the "higher" dimensions in the hierarchy cannot be reduced to an awareness of the "lower" dimensions. That is, although moral and personal awareness cannot exist apart from the physical dimension, they cannot be explained solely in terms of it either. In this way the concept of mediated dimensions can be seen to go a long way toward overcoming the dichotomy between fact and value. Since neither fact nor value can exist without the other, nor be equated with the other, it is best to conceive of them as interpenetrating and mediating dimensions.

By "physical dimension" I mean that aspect of experience in which we are aware of the material world. Although more will be said about the contextual nature of all levels of awareness in the next section, it should be pointed out here that our awareness of the physical world cannot be fully explained in terms of sensation alone. Perception involves a much greater degree of cognitive and fully integrated activity than is allowed for in the "phenomenalist" epistemology of modern empiricism. The insights and detailed work of Maurice Merleau-Ponty are especially helpful in replacing a "sense-data" or "quantum" theory of perception with a more holistic, contextual, and action-centered theory.[3] The major point that needs to be made in this connection is that the perceiving subject exists in an active relationship with that which he perceives, not in the *tabula rasa* relationship of passive observer. Thus the perceiver and the perceived exist as poles of a dynamic continuum, rather than as dichotomized, static entities.

By the term "moral dimension" I mean that aspect of experience in which we are aware of other persons. Although it is clear that one comes to know other persons as mediated through their physical existence, it is also clear that the knowledge of them cannot be reduced to an account of their physical existence. As a matter of fact, the more closely one comes to know another person, the less his knowledge is discussable in terms relating to the physical dimension. It is by means of our knowledge of other persons that we become aware of the moral dimension of existence. Here again it is important to remember that persons exist in a dynamic relationship to one another, and not as totally separate entities. Moral awareness is even more contextual and mediated than perceptual awareness. This explains why it seems more reasonable for a person to question the reality of the moral dimension than it does for him to question the reality of the physical dimension. Nevertheless, the near universality of moral awareness renders such questioning quite academic.[4]

The term "personal dimension" is meant to indicate that aspect of experience in which we are aware of ourselves as persons. Here, too, it is important to bear in mind that self-awareness is always mediated by means of the physical and moral dimensions. The necessity of the physical dimension for self-awareness should be self-explanatory. In addition to the fact that the material environment provides the necessary context for self-knowledge, it is also true that such knowledge is mediated through the knowing subject's own body. Once again it should be pointed out that to a large extent the epistemological dichotomy which is under attack in these pages is based upon a dualism between mind and body which Kant inherited from the likes of Descartes and Plato. The key to overcoming this dichotomy is a more holistic interpretation of human nature that implies a dimensional and mediational epistemology.

In spite of the fact that self-awareness must necessarily be mediated through physical and moral awareness, it must never be forgotten that it cannot be equated with, nor accounted for in terms of, those other dimensions. Although the self does not exist independently of other dimensions of experience, it does transcend them in the sense that it serves as the locus of awareness and intentional action. As Michael Novak says:

> . . .the experience of being aware is a condition of and is prior to all other experience. It is a cognitive experience, but it is not a looking, nor a reasoning, nor a reflecting. It is so simple an awareness that it is difficult to describe in words. In

describing it, one is forced to describe some other act, in which indirectly and as by a certain overriding awareness the knower is aware of his own identity even as he performs the other act. Thus one is led to distinguish two forms of awareness. First awareness is simple, indirect, unreflective. It is common to the learned and unlearned, the sophisticated and the unself-conscious. Through it, one is simply "present to oneself." One wants to say, "Me—remembering and imagining and reasoning—through all my experience, *me*."[5]

The unique and perplexing nature of self-awareness is clearly reflected in the logic of the first person pronoun, "I." Although "I" often functions like other pronouns or like proper names, it also frequently functions in a unique fashion. Thus, for instance, "I" cannot be replaced by a proper name, nor by a physical description, but can only be used by the person committing a speech-act. As Wittgenstein put it: "My own relation to my words is wholly different from other people's."[6]

The move I am advocating in this section is that of replacing the traditional realm-model of reality and experience with a dimensions-model which involves a mediating relationship between the dimensions of physical, moral, and personal awareness. One of the more stimulating and profound presentations of such a dimensional view of reality is found in Edwin A. Abbott's classic, *Flatland*.[7] Variously construed as an adventure in science fiction, as an exploration in formal mathematics, or as an essay on religion, there can be little doubt that this book well deserves the attention it has received. Although it is not set forth in a philosophical manner, the central point of Abbott's book is to make a case for viewing reality as multidimensional. Building on the concept of geometric dimensions, the book suggests the possibility of viewing the whole fabric of human experience as dimensional in nature.

The narrator of *Flatland* exists only in a two-dimensional world, but he has a vision in which he visits "Lineland," a one-dimensional world. In this vision he finds it extremely difficult to explain to the inhabitants of the new world what his own world is like. Upon returning to his own land and to "normal" experience, he is visited by a being from "Spaceland," a three-dimensional world, and though he has great difficulty understanding his visitor's way of talking about experience, he is helped immensely by recalling the difficulty he himself had trying to discuss experience with the inhabitants of one-dimensional reality. Finally, the narrator is allowed to experience the three-dimensional world and to explore its spherical mysteries for himself. Upon returning to his own Flatland, he seeks to proclaim the existence of the third dimension—whereupon he is jailed as a subversive.

I have mentioned this book here in order to provide a bridge between the previous discussion of the dimensional nature of experience and the discussion of revelation to be presented in Chapter Seven. There it will be argued that the dimensional model allows for the possibility of a religious dimension of reality which reveals itself through the mediation of the other dimensions of experience. Viewing experience as dimensional opens up the possibility of religious knowledge. The exploration of this possibility, however, will have to be postponed until a more thorough account of the nature of knowledge has been provided.

2. COGNITIVITY AS CONTEXTUAL

Given the fact that the various aspects of experience are best viewed as dimensional in their relation to one another, what is the nature of the knowing experience for the person situated within these simultaneously interpenetrating dimensions? What are the characteristics of cognitive significance; how is it grasped? The traditional model for understanding cognitive experience has nearly always been some sort of basic distinction between the known and the knower; that is, between what is "given" in experience and the mind to which it is given. This approach is clearly expressed in the position of Kant, and in recent years the empiricist variation has become increasingly influential. It is with the replacement of this traditional model by a more contextualist one that this section is concerned.

The major objection to be raised against the traditional approach, which views cognitivity as a function of the relationship between the given (the known) and the individual mind (the knower), pertains to its rigidity. To begin with, a position which attempts to speak of the two entities of the knowing situation as if they were isolated from the other aspects of experience will not jibe with the dimensional analysis set out in the foregoing section. Whatever is known participates in a variety of dimensions at the same time. With respect to the knower, it must be said that any position which seeks to view the knower as functioning with only one avenue of perception at a time is grossly inadequate. Yet this is precisely what "atomistic" and "sense-data" theories of perceptual cognition seek to do when they speak of sounds, colored patches, hardness, etc. as if each was experienced in isolation from the other. These various aspects of perceptual cognition are, in fact, experienced in concert with each other by the fully integrated sense of the knower.

One other point about the rigidity of the traditional view of cognition bears mentioning. The distinction, and ofttimes dichotomy, which is made between what is given and the one to whom it is given fails to take into account the simple fact that what is "the given" in one situation for one person may not be "the given" for another person in the same situation. This is true for all levels of experience, from physical perception to moral awareness. This fact of the relativity of cognitive significance makes it clear that what is needed is a model for understanding experience which is flexible enough to do justice to the contextual nature of experience without falling into the throes of skepticism.

It should be noted that the view of cognitivity here under attack is directly related to the picture theory of language as it was discussed at the beginning of Chapter

Four. The idea that there are isolatable "objects" of knowledge which can be experienced through the senses by a passive "observer" goes hand-in-hand with the idea that the point of language is for the observer to name the objects which he experiences so he can talk about them when they are not present. As it proved necessary to replace the picture theory of language with a more functional and contextual theory, so it appears necessary to replace the simple dualistic view of cognitive awareness with a more functional and contextual view. Although this is not the place to go into the technical aspects of such a view, it should be noted that the present discussion follows the main lines of Gestalt psychology.

Rather than thinking of cognitive significance as a static, dualistic relationship between the knower and the known, it is more helpful to think of it as a dynamic, contextual relationship in which the factors and dimensions comprising the knower and the known are subject to a good deal of fluctuation. The contextual boundaries of any situation yielding cognitive awareness are always rough and are determined by a variety of factors. Among these factors are such things as intentionality and purpose, the activity and response of both the knower and the known, and the social and perceptual conventions involved. These contexts exist against the backdrop of a vast number of overlapping continua, such as those which extend between perception and conception, between formal and informal logic, between thought and action, and between objectivity and subjectivity. Thus cognitive significance can arise in any context located anywhere on these various continua, depending upon the way the context is focused by the knowing person.

Two brief examples of the dimensional and contextual nature of cognitive significance should be sufficient. On the perceptual level consider the experience of being confronted with a puzzle-picture. Here the question of what is "given" is often quite meaningless. On the other hand, it is obvious that one cannot read into the puzzle-picture any configuration whatever. At the same time, the question concerning what a person "sees" in the picture-puzzle will depend upon a variety of factors, such as what he is told to look for, what he hopes to see, and his experience with other picture-puzzles. The contextual nature of cognitive significance is dramatically seen when, as the result of an additional clue, a person becomes aware of a pattern which had previously gone unnoticed.

On the moral level the contextual nature of cognition can be seen in considering a father's relationship to his disobedient son. Here again the father's cognition of the situation, as well as the nature of the son's act, is altered according to the dynamic development of the context. At first the father may perceive the son's disobedience as defiance. Then, in response to the words "I didn't know," he may perceive it as a mistake—or perhaps as defiance covered up by a lie. Finally, at the words "I'm sorry, dad" (uttered in the right tone and circumstances), the father is made aware of the reciprocal nature of the moral realm, for now the focus shifts to him and the possibility of forgiveness. The point is simply that our awareness of cognitive significance, on whatever level, is entirely a function of the factors comprising the context.

A thinker who has set a fast pace in the effort to reconstruct contemporary epistemology, and upon whose thought much of the present discussion is based, is Alan Pasch. In summing up his very thorough argument against the traditional view of cognitive significance, he says this:

> As the gap between the ordinary and technical kinds of significance becomes wider and empirical significance becomes more of a problem, philosophic attempts to meet the problem become more sophisticated, tend to ignore the ordinary kind of significance, and result in a further widening of the gap. The present account may be understood as seeking to restore the experientially prior kind of significance to philosophic empiricism without losing whatever benefits have been won through concern for a rigid criterion of meaning. The vehicle for the restoration is the contextualist theory of significance, which not only prevents the extreme rigidity that leads to

suspension of judgment in dealing with empirical contexts but also gives rise to a philosophic concept of significance that does justice to and is continuous with experienced significance. The concept of significance emerging from a contextualist approach is continuous with experienced significance because the latter is contextual, and rigidity is prevented because the contextualist theory is pluralistic, adapting its criteria to whatever context is to be evaluated. [8]

Pasch goes on to outline a theory of cognitivity based upon a distinction between those questions which arise within a context ("internal questions") and those which arise about the context ("external questions"). He argues that those who have sought to push the analysis of meaning down to its ultimate foundation (be it sense-data, atomic facts, objects, etc.) have failed to observe this distinction. Questions of meaning and truth can be answered, but only within a well-defined context. As the focus of attention shifts from the original question to one about the factors making up the original context, the context itself shifts. Thus there is no possibility of ever producing a complete and precise analysis of cognitive meaning in general. [9] Nevertheless, within a given context significance can be discerned, and that is all that is necessary.

Precision, like cognitive significance, tends to be pursued for its own sake. This absence of ulterior motive is harmless when precision carries clearness in its wake and when whatever has cognitive significance has empirical significance also. But the fact is that it is not maximum precision which governs our cognitive behavior but significant precision. The limit to the degree of precision we attain in low-level cognition is determined by significance in the sense in which it is experienced, which is to say, by empirical significance. We strive, in any cognitive situation, for the maximum degree of precision that is relevant or important or valuable in that situation. [10]

The thinker who has made what might well be the most lasting contribution to the construction of a "post-critical" epistemology is Michael Polanyi. Like Pasch, he has had the insight to draw several crucial distinctions (not dichotomies!) which provide guidelines for any attempt to over-come the epistemological dualism of our day. I will use one of Polanyi's basic distinctions in this section and two others in the next. Although I willingly credit Professor Polanyi with providing the direction of my thought in these two chapters, I do not want to saddle him with responsibility for the extrapolations I make from his thought.

The first of Polanyi's important distinctions upon which I wish to build is the one between "focal" and "subsidiary" awareness.[11]   In any given cognitive context there are some factors of which the knowing subject is aware because he is directing his attention to them. This Polanyi terms "focal awareness." In the same context there are also factors of which the knower is aware even though he is not focusing on them. This is "subsidiary awareness." By way of example, in the context of reading these words the reader focuses his attention on their mean-ing, not on the letters of which they are composed, nor even upon the words themselves. Nonetheless, it is obvious that the reader is subsidiarily aware of both the letters and the words.

Clearly this distinction, like all contextual distinctions, is a relative one. In other words, a person can direct his attention to those factors of which formerly he had only subsidiary awareness, thereby becoming focally aware of them. In like manner, one can become subsidiarily aware of those factors of which formerly he was focally aware. This is obvious with respect to the above example of letters, words, and meaning. It also is true about other levels of experience, such as the psychological, the moral, and possibly the religious. In all these cases the cognitive context is brought into being by the knowing subject's "attending from" that of which he is focally aware. Po-lanyi summarizes it this way:

> When we are relying on our awareness of something (A) for attending to something else (B), we are but subsidiarily aware of A. The thing B to which we are thus focally attending, is

then the meaning of A. The focal object B is always identifiable, while things like A, of which we are subsidiarily aware, may be unidentifiable. The two kinds of awareness are mutually exclusive: when we switch our attention to something of which we have hitherto been subsidiarily aware, it loses its previous meaning. Such is briefly, *the structure of tacit knowing.*[12]

The major epistemological point to be drawn from this distinction is that not only is cognitive awareness exclusively a function of contextual significance, it is a function of a continuum between focal and subsidiary awareness as well. Knowledge as awareness simply cannot be limited to that of which we are focally aware. In order for there even to be a context in which one can be focally aware of some factors, there must also be some factors of which one is only subsidiarily aware. In short, one must have a "place to stand"—to attend *from*—in order to be able to attend *to* anything at all. This contextual interpretation of cognitive awareness avoids the pitfalls of both skepticism and those positions (be they rationalistic or empiricistic) which demand indubitability. Contrary to the former, knowledge remains a realizable possibility, while contrary to the latter it does so only within flexible contexts.

3. KNOWLEDGE AS TACIT

A second distinction made by Polanyi serves well to bring out the connection between the foregoing discussion and the main theme of this section. This distinction is between the two poles of what might be called "the activity continuum." All human activity can be placed on a scale somewhere between "conceptualization," which is most often verbal, and "embodiment," which pertains to nonverbal behavior. The vast majority of human behavior is an inextricable mixture of both verbal and bodily activity. Even simple thinking (to say nothing of talking) is likely to be accompanied by certain bodily movements; alternatively, bodily action is likely to have corresponding mental (and even verbal) activity. Athletes talk to them-

selves or to their opponents; sailors and workcrews sing as
they work; and lovers feel it necessary to "whisper sweet
nothings" to each other.

There is a sense in which every activity on this continuum can be said to involve the making of a judgment. In
addition to assertions and thought processes, which obviously involve judgments, it can be shown that even such
so-called non-cognitive verbalizations as "hello" and "oh!"
imply a judgment about the situation in which they are
uttered. At the other end of the continuum, even such
almost totally bodily behavior as reflex actions imply a
judgment about the situation in which they are performed.
This is why we say that a ballplayer "misjudged" the ball,
or that a motorist "misjudged" the speed of the other car.
Any given human act is performed within a context which
renders it an act of judgment in relation to that context.

An important corollary to this "activity continuum" is
the fact that any human behavior, to the extent that it
implies making a judgment, involves a knowledge claim
and can be evaluated as either appropriate (true) or inappropriate (false). Thus there is no room for a hard and fast
distinction between "saying" as a cognitive activity and
"doing" as a non-cognitive activity. Whether a particular
act is verbal or nonverbal is always a question of degree,
but there is no question of whether or not an act implies a
cognitive judgment. To some extent all acts do.

The other side of this corollary is that all knowledge
claims involve the commitment, or "personal backing," of
the one making the claim. This will be discussed more fully
in the next chapter. The point, in short, is simply that even
though a knowledge claim is implicit in a given action, be
it verbal or nonverbal, the person involved is nonetheless
responsible for substantiating his claim. We hold people
accountable for their reflex actions as well as for their
verbal promises. All human activity is predicated upon the
reality of responsible commitment.

Now to bring these two distinctions together for the
main point of this section. The first distinction was be-

tween focal and subsidiary awareness and the second was
between conceptual and bodily activity. When these two
sets of distinctions are related to one another the result is a
third distinction between *explicit* and *tacit* knowledge.
The relationship can be visualized by imagining the
"awareness continuum" and the "activity continuum" as
dimensions which intersect each other. When the poles of
focal awareness and conceptual activity are related, the
result is "explicit knowledge." When the poles of subsidiary awareness and bodily activity are related the result is
"tacit knowledge." As every awareness and activity is a
mixture of its respective poles, so every form of knowledge
is a mixture of both explicit and tacit elements. In other
words, relating the first two continua in this way produces
yet a third continuum—the knowledge continuum—
between the explicit and tacit poles.

To put this distinction another way, every context in
which cognitive significance is present is comprised of both
tacit and explicit factors. That is, the context exists somewhere on the continuum between these two poles. The
interaction between those factors of which the subject is
focally aware and his conceptual response gives rise to
explicit knowledge. Such is the case when a person attends
to and names an object in his perceptual field. The interaction between those factors of which the subject is subsidiarily aware and his more nonverbal, bodily response
gives rise to tacit knowledge. Such is the case when the
person attending to and naming an object in his perceptual
field is not conscious of, but still must be said to know,
the functioning of his senses and discriminatory powers
which render his explicit knowledge possible. That he
knows these tacit factors can be made clear by asking him
to focus on them, whereupon he may become quite articulate about the movement of his head and hands, and about
the rational steps necessary in identifying an object. But
then, some other factors will be supplying the tacit context within which this new focusing is taking place.

Explicit knowledge, then, is the sort of knowledge with

which we are quite familiar. In fact, for all practical purposes, it is the only form of knowledge which nearly all philosophers of the Western tradition, whether rationalist or empiricist, have been willing to admit. Indeed, it is this refusal to think of knowledge as a continuum which has led to the absolute dichotomy between cognitive and non-cognitive judgments. Polanyi's continuum approach to the nature of cognitive significance is very closely related to Pasch's contextual approach. When these concepts are combined, the groundwork has been laid for the construction of a more adequate epistemology. A contextual and continuum interpretation of cognitivity allows for making relative distinctions, but avoids the necessity of establishing absolute dichotomies, between judgments of fact and judgments of value.

There are two further points about the relation between explicit and tacit knowledge which need to be discussed by way of coming to a firmer understanding of the latter. Both of these points are made in the following paragraph from Polanyi:

> Things of which we are focally aware can be explicitely [sic] identified; but no knowledge can be made *wholly explicit*. For one thing, the meaning of language, when in use, lies in its tacit component; for another, to use language involves actions of our body of which we have only a subsidiary awareness. Hence, tacit knowing is more fundamental than explicit knowing: *we can know more than we can tell and we can tell nothing without relying on our awareness of things we may not be able to tell*.[13]

Polanyi's main thesis is that tacit knowledge is not only a legitimate form of knowledge, but that it is logically prior to explicit knowledge. In any situation the subject tacitly relies upon a large variety of factors in order to know any factors explicitly. Moreover, although what is known tacitly in one context may well be known explicitly in another context, Polanyi insists that some tacit knowledge can never be known explicitly. In short, as not all words can be defined, so not all knowledge can be explicated.

What sort of things can be said to be examples of tacit knowledge? Polanyi often discusses bodily and perceptual skills as exemplifying tacit knowledge. All of us walk, swim, shoot basketballs and the like without being able to articulate this knowledge in words. In addition, we all are able to recognize another person's face in a crowd of thousands without being able to say how we do it. A more complex and much more important example of tacit knowledge is the ability to grasp the concept of "meaning." Child and philosopher alike are unable to be explicit about the meaning of the term "meaning," but it is obvious that they both know what it means. The best way of accounting for the logical primitiveness of meaning is in terms of tacit knowledge. The difficulty of the seeming circularity of the concept of meaning is similar to that which has traditionally arisen over the concept of knowledge. This latter difficulty received its classic statement in Plato's *Meno*, and as stated there provides strong substantiation for Polanyi's position on the necessity of tacit knowledge.

> . . .the *Meno* shows conclusively that if all knowledge is explicit, i.e., capable of being clearly stated, then we cannot know a problem or look for its solution. And the *Meno* also shows, therefore, that if problems nevertheless exist, and discoveries can be made by solving them, we can know things, and important things, that we cannot tell. [14]

One aspect of tacit knowledge which bears special mention is that which pertains to the role of the body. As was emphasized at the outset of this section, it is necessary to view bodily activity as a form of cognitive judgment. Another way of putting this is to maintain that our bodies function as instruments to attain knowledge which is often tacit. Thus tacit knowledge is of necessity more closely related to bodily awareness and activity. Motor knowledge, for instance, can be obtained only by means of what Polanyi calls "indwelling." The only way to know some things is to indwell or participate in them. Now, since all knowledge is to some extent tacit, it becomes apparent that indwelling is an important aspect of every cognitive situation. There is always a sense in which the process of coming to know anything, be it an object or a person, is dependent upon empathetic indwelling. As Polanyi puts it:

> We know another person's mind by the same integrative process by which we know life. A novice trying to understand the skill of a master, will seek *mentally* to combine his movements to the pattern to which the master combines them *practically*. By such exploratory indwelling the novice gets the feel of the master's skill. Chess players enter into a master's thought by repeating the games he played. *We experience a man's mind as the joint meaning of his actions* by dwelling in his actions from outside.[15]

Perhaps a summary of the discussion up to this point in this section will prove helpful. Knowledge is to be viewed as a continuum between the tacit and explicit poles. All cognitive situations involve a blending of these two polar factors. Explicit knowledge is defined as a function of focal awareness and conceptual (or verbal) activity. As such it exhibits such characteristics as precise analysis, verbal articulation, descriptive identification, observational objectivity, and an absolute distinction between the knower and the known (subject and object). Tacit knowledge, on the other hand, is defined as a function of subsidiary awareness and bodily activity. As such it exhibits such characteristics as intuitive discovery, bodily expression, holistic recognition, embodied subjectivity, and a contextual distinction between the knower and the known.

Before completing this chapter, we must indicate how the various distinctions and emphases which have been introduced are to be related to one another. The first point made was that experience and reality are best understood as composed of interacting dimensions rather than separated realms. Knowledge of the "higher" dimensions of experience, such as the moral and the personal, is mediated through the "lower" dimension of physical experience. Mediated knowledge is always dependent upon those dimensions by means of which it arises, but it can never be fully explained in terms of them. The second point made was that cognitive experience is always contextual. Thus meaning and knowledge are necessarily a function of the factors of a given situation. Moreover, cognitive experience is also a function of various levels of awareness, from the focal to the subsidiary. The final point made was that knowing is in fact a human activity, rather than a state of being. As such it involves varying degrees of bodily and verbal judgment on the part of the knower. The combination of focal awareness and conceptual activity yields explicit knowledge, while the combination of subsidiary awareness and bodily activity yields tacit knowledge. All knowledge involves a blending of explicit and tacit cognition.

The relationship between these three major points provides the conclusion toward which this chapter has been driving. The theme that ties these points together is that a fresh and adequate epistemological starting point necessitates viewing knowledge as awareness. In short, knowing must be seen as an activity or process. Furthermore, there exists an important functional connection between these three points. The fact that some dimensions of experience can be known only as mediated goes hand-in-hand with the fact that there are some aspects of experience of which one can only be subsidiarily aware. In addition, the combination of these two facts dovetails neatly with the concept of tacit knowledge. What I have been trying to establish is that our knowledge of the mediated dimensions of our experience is clearly to be classified as a form of tacit knowledge. We can only be subsidiarily aware of dimensions of experience which are of necessity mediated. Since it is precisely these dimensions about which it is most difficult to conceptualize, our cognitive response to them is primarily one of indwelling. Thus our knowledge of them is primarily tacit.

What is the significance of all this for undermining the epistemological dichotomy lying at the base of modern philosophy? By taking this dichotomy as its foundation, modern thought has found itself led into a schizophrenic stalemate which makes it necessary to choose between fact and value. However, in substituting the understanding of knowledge presented in the foregoing pages, we open the way for an appreciation of both factual and valuational judgments as cognitive acts. With a theory of knowledge that views cognition as existing on a continuum between tacit and explicit poles, it is no longer necessary to reject value judgments as non-cognitive. Clearly, our value judgments are located in the mediated awareness of the personal and moral dimensions of experience. Such awareness is no less cognitive for being tacit. This approach opens the way to explore the relationship between tacit and explicit knowledge, rather than simply rejecting either fact (as with existentialism) or value (as with empiricism) from the arena of significance.

Two final comments. It should not be thought that the foregoing epistemological theory makes it necessary to accept all claims to tacit knowledge as authentic. All that has been done is to provide a broader and more flexible model for understanding the experience of cognition. The standards whereby tacit claims to knowledge are to be evaluated will be discussed more fully in the next chapter. Further, there is, of course, an important connection between the conclusion reached in this chapter and the concern for the possibility of religious knowledge. In Chapter Seven it will be argued that this new epistemological model opens up the possibility of conceiving of religious experience as mediated by moral and personal experience in such a way as to produce a form of tacit knowledge. One further step must be added to the overall argument, however, before this case can be presented.

VI: Knowledge as Response: Commitment and Truth

At the beginning of the preceding chapter I indicated that the epistemological point of departure provided by the insights of a functional view of language could be summarized in terms of two concepts: awareness and response. The central claim of this book is that when knowledge is viewed as a dynamic interaction between these two dimensions of human experience, the foundation has been laid for overcoming the modern fact-value dichotomy. In the previous chapter we explored the theme of knowledge as awareness. The concepts of dimensional experience and contextual cognitivity were seen to broaden the concept of knowledge to include various forms of tacit knowledge. In the present chapter the theme of knowledge as response will be explored. The points of focus will be the personal, functional, and metaphorical structure of knowledge and truth.

1. KNOWLEDGE AS PERSONAL

The structure of tacit knowledge has been seen to be provided by the relation between the subsidiary and indwelling poles of the awareness and activity continua, respectively. For this reason it was necessary to discuss the activity-dimension of cognitive experience while actually focusing on knowledge as awareness. But there are other aspects of the knowledge-as-activity theme which need to

138

be dealt with in this chapter. In order to avoid as much confusion as possible, the term "response" will be used in connection with "activity" to designate those aspects which have not as yet been thoroughly discussed. The purpose of this section is to state and substantiate the claim that the understanding of cognitive experience which has been emerging from the foregoing discussion calls attention to the profoundly personal nature of knowledge.

It has been argued repeatedly throughout the last two chapters that cognitive significance is a function of the personal response of the persons involved. From the point of view of language and meaning it was seen, following Wittgenstein, that far from being some sort of entity or state, linguistic meaning is an activity. In other words people have to *use* language to accomplish certain tasks in order for it to have any cognitive significance. Further, it was seen that such uses are part of a vast, flexible network of overlapping language-games which in turn are based in the modes of human existence (forms of life). In short, there is no hard and fast distinction between language and human activity—they shade into one another.

From the point of view of language and truth it was seen, following Austin, that far from being exclusively a property of factual assertions, truth is a function of the relationship between the person and the various forces of his different speech-acts. Once again one sees the vital necessity of conceiving of cognitive significance and knowledge as based in part upon the response of the knower to his situational awareness. Indeed, it has been shown that the distinction between doing things and saying things is a relative one at best, since it is possible to "do things with words" and to say things without words. It is a particular speech-act of a particular person in a specific context which is to be judged as true or false.

The view that cognitive significance is always a function of personal activity and response also receives substantiation from the considerations of the last chapter. Throughout the discussion of the dimensions-model of experience it was implied that the awareness of various dimensions is some *person's* awareness. In like manner, if cognitive significance is contextual, there must be some *person* who "reads" the former in the latter. Tacit knowing clearly involves the response of the knower. The point here is simply that knowledge as awareness and response implies that some person is aware and responding, and thus there is what Polanyi terms "a personal coefficient" in all knowing.

There are three main aspects of the concept of the personal coefficient which must be explicated in a discussion of the response-structure of knowledge. The first is that knowledge is always somebody's knowledge, and therefore personal in nature. This point has already been mentioned several times and need not be labored here. The previous discussions of the significance of the function of the pronoun "I" (in Section Three of Chapter Four and Section One of Chapter Five) clearly underline this aspect of the personal nature of knowledge. The implied prefatory "I say" with respect to every utterance turns out to be necessary to a full understanding of linguistic activity. In the same way the implied prefatory "I know" with respect to every knowledge claim turns out to be necessary to a full understanding of cognitivity. To make a claim is, after all, a personal act. Knowing is something that persons do.

The second aspect of the concept of personal coefficient which merits discussion is also rather obvious, but nonetheless frequently neglected. There is a sense in which knowledge is impossible apart from the personal involvement of the knower. On a very simple level this is easily shown to be the case. I cannot know whether or not there are two apples in the icebox without involving myself in certain procedures, such as asking another person or looking in the icebox. On a much more complicated level, I cannot know the effects of electricity unless I place myself in a proper position to experience them, firsthand or otherwise. On an even more complex level, one cannot know another person well without becoming involved with him.

Unfortunately, philosophers and other thinkers alike have often failed to take sufficient account of the importance of personal involvement to the attainment of knowledge. Natural scientists have frequently failed to leave room for the influence of their own presence or theoretical constructs upon the situation they are observing. Heisenberg's indeterminancy principle has focused this difficulty quite clearly. Social scientists often overlook similar factors in their work. The very fact that one has focused and addressed himself to a situation, as well as the ways in which these are done, affects the nature of the knowledge thereby attained.

The importance of personal involvement is greatly multiplied when one is engaged in the struggle for self-knowledge. Here the distinction between the knower and the known, a relative distinction at best, almost completely disappears. Nevertheless, even in this case it is possible to arrive at knowledge which is useful and true; we all do it every day. The necessity of the personal coefficient, whether in so-called "objective" knowledge or in self-knowledge, is pointedly expressed in Michael Novak's concept of "intelligent subjectivity":

> Nothing is known objectively except through a knower; and a knower knows objectively only by acquiring the requisite skills, discipline, and qualities of heart and mind. Among such qualities are honesty, preference for accurate judgment over personal interest, not too much haste, avoidance of presumption, and so on. The methodological relativist seems to be correct in pointing out that the foundations of all human knowing lie in the resources of intelligent subjectivity; and that as each man is, so he will judge. There is no direct path to objectivity, through immediate contact with "naked, disguised" impressions, or with spiritual essences, or in any other way. Objectivity is the much-prized achievement of intelligent subjectivity. There is no way to objectivity other than through intelligent subjectivity. It is the knower who decides what he accepts knowing to be, and disposes himself to know.[1]

It would perhaps be helpful if before going on to discuss the third and most profound aspect of the personal side of knowledge I digressed momentarily to make a brief disclaimer. Whenever anyone these days begins talking about knowledge as being personal or subjective in structure, many philosophers become uneasy. Given the contemporary dichotomies between reason and faith, fact and value, objectivity and subjectivity, such talk usually smacks of some form of irrationalism. However, since the structure of knowledge as presented in these pages has been freed from its traditional dualistic foundations, this uneasiness is no longer necessary.

It may be best to focus the above claim in the following fashion. The personal aspect of knowledge is not introduced to function as a criterion for cognitive truth. This tack is often taken by existentialist thinkers when, after having drawn the familiar dichotomies, they maintain that value (and sometimes truth, as well) can be established only by virtue of personal commitment. Such a maneuver not only results in all the dilemmas and difficulties described in Part One of this book, but contributes to the cognitive myopia of narrow empiricists as well. I have emphasized the personal aspect of knowledge in these pages to call attention to the complex and diversified structure of the knowing experience. It is *not* being claimed that truth is determined solely by personal commitment. It *is* being claimed that cognitive experience involves personal factors which must be taken into account both when one is attempting to arrive at truth and when one is setting the criteria for truth. To quote J. L. Austin once again: "When I say 'I know', I *give others my word*: I *give others my authority for saying* that 'S is P'."[2]

The third aspect of the personal dimension of knowledge is that every effort to obtain knowledge and every claim to have found it are based in the personal commitments of the person or persons involved. Such personal commitments extend in two directions: back to the total framework within which the person stands and forward to the knowledge at which he is aiming. By total framework I mean all the thought and behavior patterns which define the person's "form of life." These patterns are both individual and cultural. Thus it is that to claim that a certain statement is true is to express an implicit value judgment about the value of truth derived from the framework within which one operates. The commitment to the superiority of truth over falsehood is not something that can be justified outside the established framework; and within it such justification is superfluous. Some commitments have to be made before any cognitive investigation can get off the ground. In this sense, knowledge is personal.

It is often urged against this emphasis on personal knowledge that it leads inevitably to subjective chaos with respect to what qualifies as true. Once again it needs to be argued that this is so only if one assumes a strong dichotomy between factual judgments (which are either true or false) and value judgments (which are neither true nor false). Skepticism results only from having defined knowledge so narrowly that nothing but absolute precision and certainty qualify. Under such restrictions knowledge would, indeed, be impossible. However, it is quite clear that knowledge is not impossible. Moreover, the mixture of personal commitment with evidence and reasoning is a reality which it is high time we acknowledged.

Personal commitments also extend forward toward the knowledge at which the knower aims. Not only does the whole of cognitive endeavor and experience involve a commitment to the possibility of knowledge, it involves a commitment to the reality of the knowable world as well. Only by making such a commitment can a person lay claim to responsible belief. Having granted that his methods and abilities are always somewhat inadequate, and having admitted that to a large extent his conceptual framework is beyond justification, the knowing subject must still go ahead and state the results of his investigation in such a way as to maintain that they represent the way things are and should be universally received. Cognitive experience and expression has meaning only if it is interpreted as a true claim about reality. Polanyi summarizes this very well:

> While compulsion by force or by neurotic obsession excludes responsibility, compulsion by universal intent establishes responsibility. The strain of this responsibility is the greater—other things being equal—the wider the range of alternatives left open to choice and the more conscientious the person responsible for the decision. While the choices in question are open to arbitrary egocentric decisions, a craving for the universal sustains a constructive effort and narrows down this discretion to the point where the agent making the decision finds that he cannot do otherwise. *The freedom of the subjective person to do as he pleases is overruled by the freedom of the responsible person to act as he must.*[3]

Another way of coming at this whole question of the personal structure of knowledge is in terms of what might be called "the cult of objectivity." Philosophers and scientists alike have been so concerned to overcome the limitations of authoritarian and individualistic epistemologies that often they have made a fetish out of objectivity. This fetish has become so persuasive and pervasive as to give a sophomoric air to vast areas of contemporary life. The emphases of the preceding chapters have the merit of pointing up the contextual relativity of objectivity without falling prey either to skepticism or to subjectivism. To maintain that all knowledge is comprised of personal commitment, and on many levels, is not to say that knowledge is impossible or that it is totally relative. It is simply an attempt to contribute to a more realistic theory of knowledge by insisting that all of the factors present in cognition be acknowledged openly.

A most interesting and convincing attack upon the cult of objectivity as it is expressed by social scientists is provided by P. T. Mackenzie.[4] He maintains that the debate over whether or not social scientists should keep their works free from value judgments is misplaced. His reason for making this claim is that the debate assumes the possibility of divesting value loaded statements of their valuational aspects; and Mackenzie maintains that such divesting is not always possible: "Value is fused into many statements about social life and can only be removed at the expense of radically changing their meaning and rendering them useless for those who study social life."[5]

Mackenzie analyzes statements about social life which involve the use of such terms as "president," "owner," and "promise," and argues that it is impossible to utter statements containing this kind of term—and it is this type which forms the very heart of social life—without committing oneself to certain valuational implications about the responsibilities and rights of the people involved. To say that Mr. Brown is president of a particular club is to say that he has certain duties and rights which *ought* to be honored. The same holds for statements about owners of property and makers of promises. The insertion of substitute terms or direct quotation marks does not obviate Mackenzie's claim because such insertions either permit the statements to do the same job as they originally did, or they do not. If they do, then the statements are not value-free, and if they do not, then the meaning of the statements has been altered.

The point of Mackenzie's argument for the theme of this section is simply that a person cannot make statements about human life without using terms which commit him personally to the value system of which these utterances are a part. At the very least a person must implicitly preface his statements with "I say," and this commits him to the value system which invests the terms of the statement with meaning. Moreover, as was mentioned earlier in this section, the act of speaking commits the speaker personally to the truth of his statement and to the conceptual framework within which it is made. In this sense the following quotation from Mackenzie applies to the natural scientists as well as to the social scientists:

> ...unless social scientists are prepared to give up making such statements as "Jones is president" they cannot claim that their writings are value-free. But if they give up making such state-

> ments they run the risk of rendering their works unimportant since this is often the sort of thing we want to know. In the social sciences what is value-free is liable to be valueless.[6]

Although space will not permit further exploration of this point, there are other philosophers who have attacked the all too neat dichotomy between factual and valuational judgments. William K. Frankena has argued that the popular distinction between "meta-ethics" and "normative ethics" is misleading if it causes one to think that meta-ethics is free from normative implications.[7] Max Black and John R. Searle have argued that, contrary to modern philosophical orthodoxy, it is possible to derive an "ought statement" from an "is statement."[8] All of these arguments point up the fact that cognitive experience cannot be explained apart from the valuational dimension of personal commitment.

2. TRUTH AS FUNCTIONAL

The next element in the concept of knowledge as response that I would like to consider is the notion of truth as functional. In order to explicate this element it will be helpful to return to the thought of the two philosophers who provided the starting point for the present epistemological reconstruction. I will first deal briefly with two hints dropped by J. L. Austin, and then I will turn to a more detailed analysis of several passages in Wittgenstein's *Philosophical Investigations*.

In his discussion of truth, Austin drops two hints which not only harmonize with the main emphases of his later thought as discussed in Chapter Four, but which provide an excellent transition from the preceding section to the concern of the present section. Over against those who have maintained that to say that a given statement is true is to do no more than assert the statement, Austin argues that while this is sometimes the case, it is not always so. There are times when the question of the truth of a second statement, namely that the first statement is true, is entirely separate from the question of the truth of the first statement. In Austin's words:

> If Mr. Q writes on a notice-board "Mr. W is a burglar," then a trial is held to decide whether Mr. Q's published statement that Mr. W is a burglar is a libel: finding "Mr. Q's statement was true (in substance and in fact)." Thereupon a second trial is held, to decide whether Mr. W is a burglar, in which Mr. Q's statement is no longer under consideration: verdict "Mr. W is a burglar." It is an arduous business to hold a second trial: why is it done if the verdict is the same as the previous finding?[9]

Regardless of whether or not one sides with Austin on the question of the superfluity of such prefatory phrases as "It is true that. . ." and "I know that. . .", it remains true that his analysis calls attention to the fact that in the cases where such phrases are used a distinct speech-act has been committed. Here again the personal commitment of the speaker can be seen to be operative in relation to the context in which the speech-act is uttered. Moreover, Austin's analysis underscores the contextual and flexible nature of the question about the truth of a given statement.

The contextual and flexible nature of questions of truth is a function of variations in purpose and precision. As Austin says:

> There are various *degrees and dimensions* of success in making statements: the statements fit the facts always more or less loosely, in different ways on different occasions for different intents and purposes. What may score full marks in a general knowledge test may in other circumstances get a gamma. And even the most adroit of languages may fail to "work" in an abnormal situation or to cope, or cope reasonably simply, with novel discoveries: is it true or false that the dog goes round the cow? What, moreover, of the large class of cases where a statement is not so much false (or true) as out of place, *inept* ("All the signs of bread" said when the bread is before us)?[10]

Thus if linguistic meaning and cognitive experience are contextual and functional in structure, it appears that truth must be seen in this way as well. This point, which only appears as a hint in Austin's work, is an important theme in the work of the later Wittgenstein. I will turn now to an analysis of this theme.[11]

One of the important issues in Wittgenstein's philosophy is the nature of a proposition. In his *Philosophical Investigations* Wittgenstein contrasts his later conception of a proposition with one that clearly resembles his own early view as set forth in the *Tractatus*.[12] Against the backdrop of a discussion of the proposition, "This is how things are," Wittgenstein states the early view. This view—View No. 1—defines a proposition as "whatever can be true or false," and thus maintains that to say "P is true" is exactly the same as saying "P." Also, "not P" is the logical equivalent of "P is false." This way of stating the matter makes it look as if the concept "proposition" is determined by the prior concepts "true" and "false." In other words, it appears that we first have a clear concept of truth and falsehood, and on this basis we decide which expressions are propositions and which are not.

Over against this view, Wittgenstein sets what he takes to be a more adequate one—View No. 2. The primary difference between the two views is this: While View No. 1 implies that the concept "true" is logically prior to the concept "proposition," View No. 2 implies that these two concepts are actually interdependent. The concept "true" is no more prior to, nor independent of, the concept "proposition" than the concept "check" is logically prior to, or independent of, the concept "king" in the statement "the king in chess is *the* piece that one can check." To say that propositions are those statements which admit of true and false judgments is simply to say that the terms "proposition," "true," and "false" are interrelated in our language. Consequently, Wittgenstein concludes this brief discussion by maintaining that what a proposition is is determined by the rules of grammar and its use in a language-game. The term "proposition" belongs to a particular language-game which also involves the terms "true" and "false." One could just as easily define the latter in terms of the former.

On the basis of this short passage it can be seen that Wittgenstein's concept of truth is consistently related to the main thrust of his overall position on philosophy, language, and meaning. It is the language-game which determines the concepts "proposition" and "true" and not the former the latter, nor the latter the former.

The question of the arbitrary nature of truth which View No. 2 seems to imply is explicitly raised by Wittgenstein himself later on.[13] This is perhaps the most crucial of all passages for coming to grips with Wittgenstein's concept of truth. It should be remarked that this passage comes in the context of a discussion of the nature and justification of rules for the use of language. As was pointed out in Chapter Four, Wittgenstein says that the justifications for a particular use of language come to an end. Ultimately one can only appeal to the established use and say, "This is simply what I do—I have no choice—this is bedrock."

In light of these and similar remarks, Wittgenstein anticipates the crucial objection of relativity: "So you are saying that human agreement decides what is true and what is false?" On the contrary, argues Wittgenstein, his insistence on use as the criterion of meaning and truth does not lead to a relativistic theory in which truth and falsehood are simply matters of agreement in opinions. "True" and "false" are parts of a language which are used in connection with statements in that language, and persons using these terms are in agreement in their use of that language. The agreement in question here is not one of opinion about matters of fact, but is rather one of activity, or "form of life."

As was mentioned earlier, there is much that is not clear in Wittgenstein's use of the phrase "form of life." But what is clear from the import of his reply to this anticipated objection is that while agreement in form of life does determine the use of language in general, and of the terms "true" and "false" in particular, this is not to be construed as an agreement which renders truth and falsehood arbitrary and relative in the usual sense of those terms. Agreement in form of life would seem to be logically prior to agreement in opinion about what is and what is not the case. In other words, agreement in form of life provides the framework within which agreement in opinion may or may not take place.

Lest one think that agreement in form of life is to be identified with agreement in definitions alone, Wittgenstein goes on to argue in the next paragraph that agreements in factual judgment also play an important part in the makeup of a form of life. Both logic and experience are involved in the form of life called "communication," just as both setting up methods for measuring and obtaining measurements are involved in the form of life called "measuring."

In yet another passage, Wittgenstein returns to the concept of truth. Amid one of his frequent polemics against the view which identifies meaning with a mental process or experience, Wittgenstein considers the presumed case of one man always guessing correctly what another man is thinking. "But what is the criterion for his guessing *right*? Well," the second man replies, "I am a truthful person and I confess that he has guessed right."[14] That is to say, the truth of one's statement about what another person is thinking is determined on the basis of the truthfulness of the latter's confession, and not upon the accuracy of the former's description of the latter's mental process. The criteria for the correctness of such guesses is the truthfulness of the confession of the person whose thoughts are being guessed. The same can be said, according to Wittgenstein, concerning the criteria for the correctness of a person's account of his own dreams.

It appears, then, that Wittgenstein is maintaining that in certain situations, namely those in which a report is being given of what one is thinking, the only criterion of truth for which it is appropriate to ask is that of the truthfulness of the person giving the report. There simply is no other alternative, least of all that of an appeal to an accurate description of a process.

Although both of Wittgenstein's statements leave a great deal unsaid, there are certain points that can be summarized before moving to a consideration of one final passage. Clearly, Wittgenstein maintains that truth is neither an abstract entity nor an independent concept characterizing propositions. On the contrary, the word "true" functions within the activity of using language (language-games) and its meaning is determined by the part it plays in this language. It is in this sense that truth and falsehood can be said to be based upon human agreement, since language is an activity which is a vital part of the way in which human beings live. The totality of the forms of human life embodies an overall agreement in both language and experience, which in turn determines the use, and thus the meaning, of such terms as "true" and "false." The use of these terms in connection with reports of thoughts and dreams is different from the use usually connected with empirical reports.

Wittgenstein returns to the problem of judgmental agreement in the final pages of the *Philosophical Investigations* when he takes up the relation of evidence to judgments about colors and the thoughts of other people. While there is general agreement (though not perfect agreement) with regard to judgments about colors and mathematical calculation, "There is in general no such agreement over the question whether an expression of feeling is genuine or not."[15] The reason for the difference would seem to be that different forms of life are involved. In the former cases there are objective standards and evidence which can be appealed to, and one can express his knowledge explicitly. In the latter case there are no objective standards and evidence, and yet, "Even here, there are those whose judgment is 'better' and those whose judgment is 'worse'." Thus the ability one has to correctly judge the genuineness of an expression of feeling appears to be a form of tacit knowledge.

Wittgenstein goes on to maintain that this type of knowledge (ability) can be learned by means of "experience." Presumably he means by trial and error, as opposed to explicit principles. It is almost impossible to render this tacit knowledge (ability) in explicit language—it must be performed, not systematized. All of this raises the crucial question in Wittgenstein's mind of the basis and/or verification of this type of knowledge. What role does evidence play, and how is a judgment of this type established as true? "Or. . .does the game *end* with one person's relishing what another does not?"[16]

Wittgenstein's answer to this question seems to run like this: Although judgments about the genuineness of an expression of emotion cannot be proved, there are consequences, or implicit predictions, of such judgments which can be observed in experience, but which cannot be articulated in a general formulation. The best that can be done is to establish a "fruitful connection" between these consequences and the judgment in question. To say that a smile was genuine on the basis of its quickness (an acceptable move) suggests that all genuine smiles are quick (a prediction is made, a consequence is drawn), which is at best fruitful, but hardly a defining characteristic of genuine smiles. "It is certainly possible to be convinced by evidence that someone is in such-and-such a state of mind, that, for instance, he is not pretending. But 'evidence' here includes 'imponderable' [*unwagbare*] evidence."[17]

The next question, raised by Wittgenstein himself, is, "What does imponderable evidence accomplish?" He maintains that even if there were imponderable evidence for a judgment about the internal chemical structure of a particular substance, the evidential character of such factors would have to be established by consequences which are capable of being weighed or evaluated. From this it becomes clear, as the German term indicates, that by "imponderable" Wittgenstein means "unweighable." In other words, imponderable evidence would accomplish nothing toward confirming this particular judgment. Only "ponderable" factors can be accepted as evidence in the language-game of the physical sciences. The same must be said for imponderable factors involved in a judgment concerning the genuineness of a painting. They are superfluous because the genuineness of the judgment can be established, and must be established, by documentary evidence.

Nevertheless, if I interpret Wittgenstein correctly, in the form of life which involves judgments about the genuineness of expressions of emotions, imponderable evidence accomplishes a great deal for the simple reason that it is all that is available! On the basis of the subtleties of glance, gesture, and tone, "I may recognize a genuine loving look, distinguish it from a pretended one. . . . But I may be quite incapable of describing the difference."[18] The reason for this inability is not a lack of words, for this obstacle could easily be overcome by inventing new words. Wittgenstein does not go on to indicate explicitly why no such description can be given, but it does not seem out of line to maintain that he wants to imply that the type of knowledge appropriate to this form of life is not reducible to propositional statements. It is more an awareness that yields a skill than it is a conceptualization that yields propositions.

Wittgenstein concludes this section by suggesting that the crucial question here is how to develop a " 'nose' for something" and use that ability to achieve certain ends. In a rather cryptic way, he argues that the very fact that we can pretend, and distinguish between pretending and genuineness, logically implies that there is such a thing as knowledge concerning such matters, which is nonetheless knowledge for being a tacit skill. "A child has much to learn before it can pretend."[19]

On the basis of this analysis I will draw some conclusions relating to the theme of this section, namely that truth is functional. First, knowledge and truth are contextual. By this I mean that according to Wittgenstein the applicability of such terms as "know" and "true" is determined on the basis of the situation, or context, being considered. In other words, apart from a fairly specific, and yet perhaps tacitly accepted, context, such terms have no meaning. The meaning of knowledge-terms is a function of the particular language-game in which they "find their home." The term "true," for example, is used in a variety of ways, each of which arises out of, and is judged according to, a concrete situation. Put non-linguistically, the point seems to be that the experiences, together with the experiential criteria, of knowing are various. This is not to say that there are no standards of knowledge and truth, but rather that these standards vary in accordance with a variety of circumstances.

Second, the context of language, including epistemological language, is determined by various "forms of life." This comment is meant to call attention to the fact that the use of various knowledge-terms is only a part of a much larger and more complicated way of life. The context of language is composed of such extra-linguistic factors as physical objects, bodily activity, and human emotions. The interrelating of these factors with language throughout our "natural history," or total experience, gives rise to the various contexts and patterns which comprise "the weave of our lives," and any attempt to analyze the meaning and use of language in general, or of knowledge-terms in particular, apart from an awareness of this interrelating is bound to be misleading. Language is part of living, and must be studied in its natural habitat to be understood.

Third, various forms of life necessitate various criteria for the applicability of knowledge-terms. This conclusion is similar to my first conclusion, but its scope is wider. There the point was that since the experiential context determines the appropriateness or inappropriateness of such terms as "knowledge" and "true," varying contexts may well necessitate varying standards of appropriateness. Here the point is that since various contexts actually constitute specific instances of more comprehensive forms of life, the broad standards for the applicability of knowledge-terms may differ from one form of life to the next. In this sense it would seem permissible to speak of more than one kind of knowledge or truth. The contrast Wittgenstein draws between the criteria for mathematical and scientific knowledge on the one hand, and the knowledge of persons and skills on the other hand, serves to substantiate this interpretation. These are different "forms of life." In addition, the point about "imponderable evidence" focuses the difference between explicit knowledge, which can be *analyzed* propositionally and confirmed by *quantitative* measurement, and tacit knowledge, which can only be *affirmed* propositionally ("I *know* she loves me") and confirmed by a *qualitative* awareness of consequences.

Fourth, this contextual view of knowledge and truth does not entail a relativistic theory of epistemology. The diverse contexts and forms of life within which knowledge-terms are used are not, in Wittgenstein's view, absolutely unrelated. On the contrary, they are loosely bound together by two main factors: purpose and experience. The strata of life-forms, language-games, and contexts are all integrated by the purpose, or intention, of the persons involved in them. Within the broad guidelines implied by the purposes of any given form of life, there are a great number of "family likenesses" among the various ways in which epistemological terms are employed. Moreover, the distinctions between various forms of life and language-games are neither precise nor rigid. In some cases the criteria for terms like "true" can be clearly specified, while in cases which are in an area overlapped by two or more language-games, the criteria cannot be clearly specified. Such cases need to be adjudicated by exploration and negotiation as they arise, not by legislation, *a priori*.

Furthermore, a case can be made for interpreting Wittgenstein as maintaining that another element which integrates the diverse life-forms and language-games, in a rough-and-ready fashion, is experience. Even in cases involving the knowledge of other persons, where measurable evidence is unavailable, he insists that "consequences" and "experience" are still necessary.[20] Whether it be by means of explicit evidence or tacit ability, the means of distinguishing between knowledge and error must be closely related to the experiential dimension.

It is clear that the main thrust of Wittgenstein's approach to the concept of truth is in harmony with the account of knowledge set out in the preceding pages. Given the foregoing account of knowledge and truth as functional, what can be said about the criteria for judging the truth of a given statement of belief? The answer to this question will serve to summarize the main theme of this section.

To begin negatively, it must be said that it is not possible to give an abstract definition of truth. No static theory can be provided which lists the defining characteristics of a true statement or belief. The language-game of determining truth is, as has been seen, far too complex and flexible to yield a specific set of criteria. Thus the traditional theories of truth, such as the coherence and correspondence theories, are not so much wrong as they are restrictively misleading. There is an aspect of adequacy in both of these traditional approaches, but both are also inadequate with respect to certain situations. Moreover, there is a definite similarity between the account of knowledge and truth here presented and a sophisticated form of pragmatism.

The first positive point that needs to be made is that truth is a function of the full cognitive experience of the knowing persons involved. I use the term "full" to serve as a reminder that cognitive experience involves all dimensions of human awareness, from the physical to the personal and moral—and even, possibly, to the religious. What is true, then, is whatever is appropriate to, fits with, or harmonizes with the context within which it is maintained. Thus truth, like meaning and knowing, is entirely contextual and functional in nature. In relation to the physical dimension, the correspondence theory of realism usually proves quite workable, while in relation to the personal and moral dimensions of experience, the coherence and pragmatic theories must be brought to bear as well.

This positive point is clearly stated and substantiated by the following quotation from Robert Jordan's excellent analysis "To Tell the Truth":

> . . .whenever the alleged fact is a state of affairs involving the spatio-temporal and something more. . .whenever what is being stated has a meta-empirical element, in which case the language used be in some degree extraordinary, then the notion of correspondence is strained beyond its capacity for useful service.
>
> The reason for this is, I think, that the tense is different and the situation is dynamic and often unstable. I propose, then, to consider truth as the coming together of the word and the act where the words "coming together" are to be taken as referring to the awareness of the coincidence of word and reality, of logos and being. And although the objective coincidence is, I would hold, the primary meaning of truth, I would, for the moment, place the emphasis upon the often prolonged experience which gives rise eventually to the apprehension of that coincidence. The reason for placing the emphasis on awareness as a developing apprehension is that extraordinary statements have to be acted out or *enacted* before they can be seen, in the full sense, to be true. Furthermore, since these statements have no straightforward look-and-see-and-no-nonsense verification, we must consider, sometimes at least, whether they are consistent with other propositions which we know or which we take to be true.[21]

Jordan goes on to illustrate the functional view of truth by providing an analysis of what would be involved in verifying the statement, "My wife and I love each other." He concludes that the statement

> . . .looks backward to the past and forward to the future. It involves commitment, promises, vows, intentions, desires, hopes,—some of which will have been repeatedly weakened or even broken. . . . The statement is, in short, a most complicated and paradoxical coming together of words once spoken, of acts once done, and of the word now spoken and the act now intended. To speak of the truth of this proposition is to enact it in memory, in imagination and in deed and to find in the apparently ambiguous evidence and the conflicting claims from both sides a coherent meaning and a firm reality.[22]

Once again the value of viewing an aspect of cognitive experience according to a continuum-model, rather than according to a dichotomy-model, makes itself apparent. The criteria by means of which truth is determined turn out to be as flexible as the contexts within which cognitive experience arises. In contexts where the physical dimension predominates, precision and deductive predictability can and should be aimed at. As contexts move up the scale toward the increasing complexity of various dimensions of experience, the amount of precision and verification which are possible and necessary decreases. At the moral and personal level the criteria for truth are primarily tacit. Thus the most that can be sought in such contexts is some form of "intersubjectivity," which stands midway between traditional subjectivity and objectivity.[23]

The tacit beliefs and criteria which comprise our forms of life on the "higher" dimensions of experience can never be made fully explicit, and thus can never be strictly evaluated. However, these tacit factors are "displayed" or revealed indirectly by means of our linguistic and behavioral patterns. That is to say, they can be brought to the threshold between subsidiary and focal awareness so as to be articulated indirectly. To oversimplify, we can discern the structure of tacit truth as mediated through the contradictions and perversions that result when certain phenomena and principles are ignored. Such is the status of the justification of belief in the laws of inference, the reality of the external world, the reality of other minds, and our own selfhood. As will be seen in the next chapters, it may even be possible to maintain that the justification of one's belief in God has a similar status. All tacit claims and commitments must be evaluated in terms of their ability to provide a coherent and fruitful means for man to relate himself to experience by way of satisfying his needs.

3. METAPHOR AS COGNITIVE

Knowledge has been seen to arise from a response of personal commitment to an awareness of experiential dimensions with flexible contexts. Thus knowledge and truth are tacit and functional in their structure. This view of knowledge carries with it clear-cut implications for the question of the nature of language. Most of these implications were spelled out in some detail in Chapter Four, but one further point needs to be considered here, namely the question of the cognitive status of metaphorical language.

The implications of the case for tacit knowledge with respect to the cognitivity of metaphorical language militate against two equally inadequate and extreme interpretations. On the one hand stands the position which views metaphor as nothing but rhetorical ornamentation that can be eliminated without any loss of cognitivity. This view is dominant among empiricist philosophers, and was evident in the discussion of Paul Edwards' approach in Chapter One. It should be obvious why the functional view of language, knowledge, and truth argued for throughout these pages is opposed to such an interpretation. In brief, it is simply too closely related to the picture theory of language and the fact-value dichotomy to be able to do justice to the contextual and multi-dimensional nature of cognitive experience.[24]

At the other extreme stands the position which views metaphor as a panacea for all cognitive ills. This view is dominant among existentialist philosophers, and was in evidence in our discussion of Paul Tillich's thought in Chapter One. The move in this interpretation is simply to place all talk of value and mystery under the classification of metaphor, and then to maintain that metaphorical language is "above" normal cognitive criteria. This "above" can mean either that metaphor is non-cognitive, or that it has its own unique cognitive criteria. Those who maintain the former find themselves in basic agreement with empiricists such as Edwards, while those who maintain the latter find themselves hard pressed to indicate what the unique cognitive criteria of metaphor are. The limitations of both approaches are implied throughout Part One. In short, this whole interpretation smacks of wanting one's cognitivity without being willing to pay the price of some sort of experiential criteria.

The interpretation of metaphor as cognitive that is derived from a functional view of language and knowledge stands between these two extreme positions. Although meaning and truth are not confined to precise language about the physical dimension of experience, they are not to be assigned to every mysterious or paradoxical utterance. The cognitivity of any given metaphor must be established in relation to the context within which it is used. Although no formula can be constructed to serve as the standard for distinguishing between cognitive and non-cognitive metaphors, it does not follow that no such distinction can be made. As in the case of cognitive significance in general, metaphorical cognitivity must be seen as a function of the subject's awareness of and response to the multi-dimensional and contextual structure of experience. The truth of a given metaphor must be determined on the basis of the interrelation between the context, the speaker's intention, and the levels of awareness.

In many ways this view of the cognitivity of metaphor receives its most profound statement in the writings of the philosopher Max Black.[25] Black rejects both what he terms the "substitution view of metaphor" (that it can be replaced by a literal expression) and the "comparison view of metaphor" (that it is essentially a simile). Both of these views fail to account for the irreducible and fruitful nature of metaphorical speech. Black makes a strong case for what he calls the "interaction view of metaphor." He maintains that the significance of a metaphor is that it brings together two dimensions of experience in such a fresh way as to alter our understanding of both. The languages of the two dimensions interact in a way which "filters and transforms" each of them. Black's own summary is worth quoting in full:

> (1) A metaphorical statement has two distinct subjects—a "principal" subject and a "subsidiary" one.

(2) These subjects are often best regarded as "systems of things," rather than "things."

(3) The metaphor works by applying to the principal subject a system of "associated implications" characteristic of the subsidiary subject.

(4) These implications usually consist of "commonplaces" about the subsidiary subject, but may, in suitable cases, consist of deviant implications established *ad hoc* by the writer.

(5) The metaphor selects, emphasizes, suppresses, and organizes features of the principal subject by implying statements about it that normally apply to the subsidiary subject.

(6) This involves shifts in meaning of words belonging to the same family or system as the metaphorical expression; and some of these shifts, though not all, may be metaphorical transfers. (The subordinate metaphors are, however, to be read less "emphatically.")

(7) There is, in general, no simple "ground" for the necessary shifts of meaning—no blanket reason why some metaphors work and others fail.[26]

It is in the interaction between conceptual systems or linguistic usage that the cognitive feature of metaphor is to be recognized. As was pointed out at the close of Chapter Four, Black maintains that "interaction-metaphors are not expendable."[27] Both the user and the hearer must be aware of the interaction of dimensions which takes place, and both must grasp the insight which the interaction creates. Such awareness and grasping are cognitive activities of the first order. On this basis it can be concluded that properly used metaphorical language is not only cognitive, but is peculiarly suited to the communication of knowledge discerned on the moral and personal levels of experience. Mediated knowledge is best spoken of by means of metaphorical language, since it too is the result of interaction between dimensions.

Black approaches the question of the cognitive necessity of metaphor from another direction when he discusses the role of models in scientific theory. He distinguishes three related models: the "picture" model, the "analogue" model, and the "theoretic" model.[28] Although there are similarities among these three, the analogue model is taken to be more flexible and functional than the picture model, and the theoretic model is taken to be more comprehensive than—in fact it encompasses—the analogue model. Moreover, theoretic models "are not literally constructed: the heart of the method consists in *talking* in a certain way." This difference is not, however, to be interpreted as rendering theoretic models "merely verbal" since "if there is a change in manner of expression and representation, there is also the alleged depiction of a specific object or system, inviting further investigation."[29] Incidentally, Black, like Polanyi, insists that the persons who actually use analogue or theoretic models, and this includes nearly everyone, do not use them as "convenient conventions." While it is often claimed that models are used "as if" they referred to reality, Black maintains that a consideration of what actually happens reveals that models are used "as being" related to reality.[30]

In addition to arguing for the pragmatic value of using theoretic models, Black takes a strong stand against the position which contends that the fact that models may lead to fruitful results is simply a matter of psychology, and thus has no philosophical value. I will quote his reply to this criticism in full:

> This objection treats the relation between the model and the formal theory by which it is eventually replaced as *causal*; it claims that the model is no more than a *de facto* contrivance for leading scientists to a deductive system. I cannot accept this view of the relation between model and theory. We have seen that the successful model must be isomorphic with its domain of application. So there is a rational basis for using the model. In stretching the language by which the model is described in such a way as to fit the new domain, we pin our hopes upon the existence of a common structure in both fields. If the hope is fulfilled, there will have been an objective ground for the analogical transfer. For we call a mode of investigation rational when it has a rationale, that is to say, when we can find reasons which justify what we do and that allow for articulate appraisal and criticism. The putative isomorphism between model and field of application provides such a rationale and yields such standards of critical judgment.

We can determine the validity of a given model by checking the extent of its isomorphism with its intended application. In appraising models as good or bad, we need not rely on the sheerly pragmatic test of fruitfulness in discovery; we can, in principle at least, determine the "goodness" of their "fit."[31]

This concludes my case for tacit knowledge, which has been offered as a replacement for the dichotomized epistemology underlying contemporary thought. Taking a functional view of language as a point of departure, I have argued for a view of knowledge which focuses on dimensional-contextual awareness and personal-functional response. Finally, I have concluded that this interpretation of knowledge as tacit necessitates viewing metaphorical language as cognitive. The overall thesis of Part Two has been that the concept of tacit knowledge overcomes the limitations of the fact-value dichotomy which plagues modern philosophy.

Throughout the first two parts of this book, the background against which the structure of knowledge has been explored is the issue of the possibility of religious knowledge. Given the view that tacit knowledge is a necessary and legitimate aspect of cognitive experience, the question of religious knowledge can now be approached from a direction that was not possible under the strictures of a dichotomized epistemology. It is time to make such an approach.

Part Three

THE IMPLICATIONS:
THE POSSIBILITY OF
RELIGIOUS KNOWLEDGE

VII: Knowledge by Revelation: Mediated and Tacit

In no sense should these next two chapters be construed as attempting to provide a final answer to all the major questions of revelation and theology. All I can hope to do is present the main lines of emphasis which seem to me to follow from the foregoing epistemological reconstruction. In this chapter the concept of revelation will be related to the dimensional and contextual interpretation of cognitive experience developed in Chapter Five. In addition I will offer an interpretation of religious knowledge based on the interaction between awareness and response. The final section will deal with the question of confirming claims to religious knowledge. In the next chapter I will discuss the nature of theology as a linguistic activity. On the basis of the case for the cognitivity of metaphorical language, I will explore the function of talk about God, arguing that theological language is best understood as an effort to communicate about the awareness of a religious dimension of experience in terms of a qualified use of the language most often used in connection with other dimensions. I hope that the approach embodied in these two chapters will provide a basis for the possibility of religious knowledge which is adequate from both philosophical and the theological perspectives.

1. THE RELIGIOUS DIMENSION

In Chapter Five a case was argued for attempting to understand experience in terms of the model of simultaneously interpenetrating dimensions. This model was offered as a replacement for the traditional model of a hierarchy of isolated realms. The difference between these two ways of viewing experience and reality is especially crucial with respect to the question of revelation. The more traditional realm-model forces one to conceive of revelation as something which comes from a realm which is totally distinct from, and in some sense foreign to, our own world. Thus when the question of identifying revelation arises, the religious person is forced either to maintain the necessity and reality of miraculous events and/or infallible communications (since these alone can serve as marks of the divine realm), or to give up the claim that revelation takes place. In the latter case religion becomes identified with humanism, while in the former it becomes identified with the bizarre. The realm-model offers little if any place to stand between these two alternatives.

The dimension-model, on the other hand, makes it possible to conceive of revelation as the mediation of the religious dimension through the other dimensions of experience. Moreover, this way of viewing experience is more in line with the way the various aspects of reality are, in fact, experienced. The physical, moral, personal, and religious aspects of life are not experienced as separate blocks or compartments, but as vitally interrelated areas of concern and focus. Thus to conceive of experience as dimensional in structure is in harmony both with cognitive experience and with the possibility of a more adequate conception of revelation. This would indicate that the first step toward understanding religion and theology is to think of man as existing within a multi-dimensional universe where knowledge of the various dimensions, especially the religious dimension, is mediated through the others.

To my mind the thinker who has developed this dimensional view of religious experience most fruitfully is John Hick. A presentation of his thought on this subject should clarify my own view. Hick addresses himself to the question of how religious knowledge is possible by maintaining

> . . .that "mediated" knowledge, such as is postulated by this religious claim, is already a common and accepted feature of our cognitive experience. To this end we must study a basic characteristic of human experience, which I shall call "significance," together with the correlative mental activity by which it is apprehended, which I shall call "interpretation." We shall find that interpretation takes place in relation to each of the three main types of existence, or orders of significance, recognized by human thought—the natural, the human, and the divine; and that in order to relate ourselves appropriately to each, a primary and unevidenceable act of interpretation is required which, when directed toward God, has traditionally been termed "faith." Thus. . .while the object of religious knowledge is unique, its basic epistemological pattern is that of all our knowing.[1]

Hick uses the term "significance" to refer to that which gives order, or intelligibility, to the whole of experience. It involves the ability to differentiate between, and gather together, the various particulars of experience. Indeed, it might be defined as the very capacity to have what we call human experience. Hick seems to be saying that this "significance" is objective in that it is "built in" to the very structure of experience. Another way to characterize it is to call it that quality which enables the various aspects of experience to be brought into focus, reorganized, compared, and contrasted. The similarities between this concept of significance and the contextual view of cognitive awareness developed in Chapter Five should not go unnoticed.

The concept of "interpretation" is introduced by Hick to specify the subjective correlate of significance. It represents the activity, or response, of the mind in perceiving, or becoming aware of, significance in experience. On the object level, for instance, one becomes aware that the sense datum of his present experience can be interpreted, or responded to, in a variety of ways—as, for example, a red patch, a red thing, and a red book. Interpretations of significance in the various aspects of experience can occur on increasingly inclusive levels, depending on the extent and nature of one's past experience. Thus, to use Hick's example, a piece of paper with writing on it will be one thing to an illiterate savage, quite another to a literate person who does not know that particular language, and still another to someone who does know the language. In each case the person involved can be said to perceive both what the previous person does and something more as well. Here again there are obvious similarities between Hick's "interpretation" and the emphasis on knowledge as response in Chapter Six. It is here that personal commitment comes into play, as has been repeatedly pointed out. On the religious level, such commitment or interpretation is termed "faith."

Hick goes on to suggest that this pattern of significance-interpretation works itself out on three levels of human experience, namely the object level, the personal (or moral) level, and the religious level. The significance of personal experience is mediated through, but is not reducible to, object-significance. In like manner, the significance of religious experience is mediated through, but is not reducible to, object and personal experience.

> Our inventory, then, shows three main orders of situational significance, corresponding to the threefold division of the universe, long entertained by human thought, into nature, man, and God. The significance for us of the physical world, nature, is that of an objective environment whose character and "laws" we must learn, and toward which we have continually to relate ourselves aright if we are to survive. The significance for us of the human world, man, is that of a realm of relationships in which we are responsible agents, subject to moral obligation. This world of moral significance is, so to speak, superimposed upon the natural world, so that relating ourselves to the moral world is not distinct from the business of relating ourselves to the natural world but is rather a particular manner of so doing. And likewise the more ultimately fateful and momentous matter of relating ourselves to the divine, to God, is not distinct from the task of directing ourselves within the natural and ethical spheres; on the con-

trary, it entails (without being reducible to) a way of so directing ourselves.

In the case of each of these three realms, the natural, the human, and the divine, a basic act of interpretation is required which discloses to us the existence of the sphere in question, thus providing the ground for our multifarious detailed interpretations within that sphere.[2]

As the last sentence of this quotation makes clear, Hick is concerned to point out that even on the physical (object) level of experience an act of interpretation is needed before any significance can be apperceived. Until some active, organizing response is made, one does not have "experience" at all, only a "booming, buzzing confusion." Logically speaking, even a solipsistic interpretation of experience as a dream is a live option, and is by nature an interpretive act. Thus our disposition to interpret the sense-data of our experience in terms of the point of view of realism is pragmatically, but not logically, necessary. In a word, it is part of our form of life.

The apperception of significance on the moral level of experience is very similar to that on the physical level. A sense of moral obligation is the result of an interpretive response to an awareness of the significance of personal experience. It is, of course, possible to be unaware of, or to refuse to respond to, the significance of personal experience, and thereby fail to sense moral obligation. Such a situation is, in reality, simply giving another interpretation to personal experience. The difference between the interpretive apperception of physical and moral significance is this: It is less difficult to refuse to interpret personal experience as having moral significance than it is to refuse to interpret sensory experience as having physical (or real) significance. Nonetheless, for most human beings, moral interpretation is also part of the human form of life.

Hick is especially interested in the relation of mediation existing between the physical and moral levels of significance. He maintains that moral significance is mediated through physical experience in such a way as to be dependent on it, but not reducible to it. Moral obligation is sensed *in* the experience of physical situations, but is clearly more than an objective description of such situations would indicate. It is important to note this, since the same relation is held to exist between the apprehension of religious significance and moral and physical experience. Hick argues:

> Has this epistemological paradigm—of one order of significance superimposed upon and mediated through another—any further application? The contention of this essay is that it has. As ethical significance interpenetrates natural significance, so religious significance interpenetrates both ethical and natural. The divine is the highest and ultimate order of significance, mediating neither of the others and yet being mediated through both of them.
>
> Thus the primary religious perception, or basic act of religious interpretation, is not to be described as either a reasoned conclusion or an unreasoned hunch that there is a God. It is, putatively, an apprehension of the divine presence within the believer's human experience. It is not an inference to a general truth, but a "divine-human encounter," a mediated meeting with the living God.[3]

Such an apprehension of mediated, divine presence results in a total interpretation of all of human experience in terms of the religious dimension. This interpretation is not based on some knowledge of "outside reality," but is rather a perspective which a religious person takes toward the totality of his experience. Hick offers a reason why religious experience and knowledge have the rather open-ended structure that has been outlined above. His suggestion is that only this type of mediated structure safeguards human freedom and responsibility in relation to the religious dimension.[4] Any other structure would either make religious belief necessary or would render it impossible. The concept of mediated knowledge avoids the extremes of infallibility and skepticism.

To the crucial question "What induces a man to experience the world religiously?", Hick says:

The general nature of the answer is I think clear enough. Religious interpretations of human experience arise from special key points within that experience which act as focuses of religious significance. These key-points both set going the tendency of the mind to interpret religiously and also act as patterns guiding the forms which such interpretations take. Among the infinite variety of life's phenomena some moment or object or person stands out as uniquely significant and revealing, providing a clue to the character of the whole. Some item of experience, or group of items, impresses the mind so deeply as to operate as a spiritual catalyst, crystallizing what was hitherto a cloud of relatively vague, amorphous feelings and aspirations, and giving a new and distinctive structure to the "apperceiving mass" by which we interpret our stream of experience.

In Christianity the catalyst of faith is the person of Jesus Christ. It is in the historical figure of Jesus the Christ that, according to the Christian claim, God has in a unique and final way disclosed himself to men.[5]

In this way the historical personality of Jesus Christ serves as the key point in experience for interpreting religious significance in terms of Christian theism. It is through the personality and activity of Jesus Christ that religious significance is uniquely mediated to Christians. There are, of course, other catalysts which serve a similar purpose in other religious traditions. The question of the function of a catalyst in focusing cognitive significance will be discussed in more detail shortly.

Given this understanding of the relationship between the religious dimension and the other dimensions, it is both possible and helpful to conclude that revelation is mediated in structure. That is to say, rather than being a communication from another realm (as with Barthianism) or an encounter which transcends the other dimensions of life (as with Bultmannianism), revelation is best viewed as an awareness of another dimension of reality being mediated through the more familiar dimensions. Thus in and through his everyday experience the religious person becomes aware of the activity of another, in many ways more essential, dimension to which he responds with his total being.

This understanding of revelation as mediated is clearly related to what theologians have usually termed "general" revelation. By means of his relation to the natural and moral dimensions of reality, each person is in a position to become aware of the religious dimension. However, it is my contention that the notion of revelation as mediated is also the key to the question of the relation of revelation to history. Although this is not the place to begin a detailed discussion of what theologians usually term "special" revelation, perhaps I can give some indication of how the concept of mediated revelation provides a fresh approach to the question.

As I indicated briefly in Chapter One, the question of the relation of revelation to history is at the center of the contemporary theological stage. Traditional orthodoxy claims that revelation has taken place in the historical person of Jesus of Nazareth in such a way as to enable men with open minds to read it quite clearly. The signs given in the life and teachings of Jesus provide a straight and unambiguous line of connection between God and man. The more modern, existentialist-influenced position claims that revelation takes place in the personal encounter between the man of faith and the spirit of the living Christ in such a way as to render the historical Jesus relatively unimportant. The signs given in the life and teachings of Jesus provide a symbolic and ambiguous presentation of God's relation to man, a presentation which can be grasped only by one who already possesses faith.

Thus the distinction between the traditional and modern views of the relation of history to revelation exhibits the dichotomy between the factual and the valuational that is so basic to modern theology. The traditional view tends to identify the meaning of revelation with historical fact, while the modern view tends to isolate religious meaning from historical fact. The one asserts the existence of two realms, and maintains that revelation provides a ladder of connection between the two. The other denies the existence of more than one realm, and then maintains that revelation provides a way of viewing the one realm in a meaningful fashion. Both points of view accept without question the dichotomy between the realms of fact and value, with each seeking to maintain the superiority of the one over the other.[6]

Into this situation comes the concept of revelation as mediated by the interaction between the various dimensions of experience. Such a concept begins by denying the realm-model which serves as the foundation for both of the foregoing views, and it ends by avoiding the schizophrenic stalemate to which these views lead. The crux of the difference between this view and those discussed above lies in the term "mediation." Given the epistemological reconstruction presented in Chapters Five and Six it is no longer necessary to view cognitive awareness as direct and "objective," nor as devoid of valuational significance. Value and existential meaning are mediated by the factual and historical dimensions of human experience. Thus there is no need either to identify value with fact and revelation with history, or to isolate them from one another. As Henri Bouillard says about the relationship between revelation and historical signs:

> But note that these signs are not the middle term in a line of reasoning that would inevitably lead to the conclusion that God has actually revealed himself. They are the place or juncture in which we experience, the transparency (so to speak) in which we perceive, the revelation God is making to us. The point at which they mediate is the point of immediate contact between God as he reveals himself and the surge of faith that rises to meet him in the revelation. We do not reason from the signs to the revelation; we read the revelation in the signs.[7]

There is some evidence that contemporary theology is moving in the direction of a concept of revelation as mediated. First off there is the "New Quest" movement among Bultmann's disciples, which seeks to go beyond him by looking to the speech-events of Jesus as mediators of Christian revelation. Both Ernst Fuchs and Gerhard

Ebeling display a more dimensional and contextual under-standing of language and history than does either Barth or Bultmann.[8] In addition there is the rising influence of Wolfhart Pannenberg, who is likewise insisting on the crucial importance of history as a mediator of revelation. The context[9] of the following quotation from Pannenberg makes it clear that he is seeking to overcome the same dichotomy as we have attacked throughout this present volume:

> Revelation is not the starting point, but the end of a long path, which began with still indistinct and inadequate notions of God. It is not true that the revelation, the self-disclosure of God, falls from heaven ready-made. Nor must it be the starting point of all knowledge of God, as if one could not otherwise know anything about him. There is rather, speaking metaphor-ically, a veiled God in the beginning, and only in the end is the veil taken away, i.e., the *re-vel-atio* takes place. Men could not endure a nonmediated confrontation with the actuality of God. To do so they would have to be something other than creatures who seek their way by orientation to finite things. Men can approach God only through the world of finitude. Through the veil of the finite, men become aware of the infinite God. Therefore their perspective is always one-sided and distorted. But at the end of the veiled way revelation from God can occur, the self-unveiling of the God already pro-visionally known through all the obscurities of the veiling. The self-unveiling of God, however, is salvation to mankind be-cause only in God's proximity, in community with God, does human existence find its fulfillment.[10]

2. RELIGIOUS KNOWLEDGE AS AWARENESS AND RESPONSE

With the dimensional and mediational structure of reli-gious experience firmly established, it is now necessary to discuss its two-fold contextual nature in terms of aware-ness and response. The basic thrust of the claim to reli-gious knowledge is that the person involved discerns (by means and in the midst of his everyday experience in the physical and moral dimensions of life) yet another dimen-sion of reality which enriches his understanding of the more common dimensions. The discernment which takes place in such a disclosure especially enhances the person's moral sensitivity and his own self-understanding. In response to this disclosure-discernment situation, which corresponds to the "awareness continuum" discussed in connection with Polanyi's thought, the person's life becomes characterized by a profound sense of commitment which penetrates every aspect of his behavioral and conceptual existence. This response corresponds to the "activity continuum" discussed in connection with Polanyi's position.

Within the fabric provided by various cognitive contexts, the religious person discerns and responds to a dimension of reality which mediates itself through the other dimensions as that which gives existence and meaning to them. In this sense the religious person maintains that this new dimension is ultimate or "divine." Of course, for the Christian the life and teachings of Jesus are taken to provide the context within which this ultimate dimension of reality is most clearly focused. Although not every context actually does disclose the religious dimension, every context would seem to be capable of such disclosure. Religious discernment and commitment can occur on all levels and in all aspects of human experience.

No one has done more to explicate the two-fold contextual structure of religious experience as awareness and response than Ian Ramsey, the present Bishop of Durham and formerly professor at Oriel College, Oxford. Beginning by laying the groundwork of contextual disclosures which are not religious in nature, he proceeds to build a most helpful vantage point from which to appreciate the possibility and structure of religious disclosure.

In his *Religious Language*, Ramsey develops examples of disclosures which take place within perceptual, especially visual, experience. Here he draws heavily upon the work of Gestalt psychology.

> Let us recall how there could be drawn twelve straight lines which at first sight might look no more than two squares with

corners joined. But then there dawns on us "depth," and we see the twelve straight lines as a "unity." The lines indeed represent a cube and this cube may, as is well known, seem to enter into or stand out of the surface on which the lines are drawn. Here again is a characteristically different situation which dawns on us at some recognizable point. This is the point where twelve straight lines cease to be merely twelve straight lines, when a characteristically-different situation is evoked which needs odd words like "depth" and "unity," or mathematically the idea of a "new dimension," "volume" besides "area."[11]

In other contexts, Ramsey mentions the recognition of an old friend, the rearrangement of pieces in a puzzle, and the way in which a series of polygons of an increasing number of sides may suggest a circle, as examples of perceptual situations that give rise to a disclosure which involves a dimension other than the sum of the particulars. This sort of example reminds one of Wittgenstein's discussion of seeing a particular picture "as" a duck or "as" a rabbit.[12]

The realms of mathematics and science are seen by Ramsey as involving disclosures which might be termed theoretic. The way in which the axioms of Euclidean geometry, for instance, are "seen" as "self-evident" by the beginning student suggests a conceptual understanding that goes beyond simply understanding the meaning of the sentence involved.[13] Although Ramsey does not mention them, it seems that one could offer the grasping of the rules for deductive and inductive inference as further examples of theoretic situations in which a special discernment is implied. One other example which Ramsey borrows from mathematics is the way in which the concept of "infinite" is delineated in the use of such phrases as "infinite sum."[14] Although it bears certain similarities to other sums, it can never be fully explained in terms of them. From observing its use in actual situations one "discerns" what it means. Perhaps the same could be said for the symbol "zero."

Elsewhere, Ramsey goes to some length to establish the fact that in the construction of scientific hypotheses and laws, the scientist makes use of disclosures which go beyond the data at hand.[15] In the former instance, the scientist often conceives a causal pattern among various phenomena on the basis of an extremely small amount of data. Moreover, even when the hypothesis thus conceived has been confirmed by a vast amount of data, the resultant "law" is still only a highly refined generalization which needs to be qualified by talk about "normal conditions" and "experimental error." The point is that in making such a generalization, the scientist is giving expression to a discernment which is based in, and yet goes beyond, the actual facts. This same sort of analysis would seem to shed some light upon the contemporary debate about the justification of induction, if such justification were seen as the justification of an insight.

Moving on to examples of disclosure which are humanistically more significant, it is important to examine what may be called moral discernment. Ramsey uses such examples because he is convinced that the most significant disclosures religiously are those which center in personal and inter-personal relationships. In a review of a lecture on "Reason and Experience in Ethics,"[16] he takes a definite stand against the tendency in contemporary ethics to segregate ethical discourse from other uses of language as *sui generis*. He maintains that moral judgments must be based in, and thus are closely related to, the judgments of psychology and sociology. It is impossible for ethical discourse to take place in a vacuum. Nevertheless, ethical judgments cannot be reduced to factual judgments. This dilemma, which forms the very heart of contemporary ethical debate, can be overcome only by acknowledging that ethical judgments result from disclosures which go beyond, but are not independent of, the factual elements of a given situation. When a duty is discerned, or an ethical judgment is made, a disclosure has been mediated by the spatio-temporal facts; a disclosure which, although common in everyday experience, is not exhaustible in terms of straightforward, descriptive language.

Ramsey illustrates his point with the example of a man sweeping up litter and coming across a letter written by his son or daughter. The moral question of whether or not the man should read the letter can be decided only by considering all the facts of the situation.

> We recognize something as an obligation and duty, when. . .it presents itself to us within a disclosure situation. But it is notorious that there can be "conflicts" of duty—the Hampstead Heath sweeper may think he has a duty to exert a protective providence over his son or his daughter; equally well a duty to respect his or her privacy. We then have the prospect of a disclosure presenting us with two challenges which generate conflicting responses. The only way to resolve the difficulty is to develop the empirical details in each case until there arises within the one disclosure a single challenge and response.[17]

Ramsey offers as another example of a disclosure situation the sense of moral obligation a bystander experiences when a child is drowning.[18] A purely physical description of the situation does not exhaust the sense of duty. In fact, it would always be possible to say, "Well, there goes another blob of protoplasm." Nevertheless, it is just as true that the sense of duty does not occur apart from a cognition of the facts.

Similarly, our knowledge of other persons, *qua* persons, involves a disclosure which arises out of, but cannot be equated with, our knowledge and talk of their behavior. Since this aspect of experience is integral to morality, it is appropriate to discuss it at this juncture. One can think of examples of how we come to know other persons—and become aware that they are more than the sum total of their physical behavior—by the introduction of one additional fact which serves to integrate and give depth to all the other facts we know about the person. There are striking, and unaccidental, parallels between what Ramsey has to say on this subject and what philosophers Gilbert Ryle and P. F. Strawson have to say about the problem of knowing other minds.[19] In each case there is an emphasis on the fact that our knowledge of other persons "goes beyond" our knowledge of their behavior, not in the sense that an inductive hypothesis goes beyond the data, but in the sense that we *begin* and do not conclude, by speaking and behaving towards others as persons. In Strawson's terminology, this is one of the senses in which the concept of person can be said to be "logically primitive."

Perhaps the most illuminating illustration Ramsey gives of the type of disclosure involved in knowing other persons is an imaginary conversation between Robin Hood and the Tinker who was out to arrest him.

> The Tinker unexpectedly meets Robin Hood and the conversation proceeds like this:
> Q. Do you know Robin Hood?
> A. Oh, very well indeed, I have the closest knowledge of him.
> Q. Where is he now, I wonder?
> A. I am sure he cannot be very far away.
> Q. Is he strong?
> A. Fairly so. He had a successful bout with a very skilled wrestler the other day.
> Q. How tall is he?
> A. Just about my height.
> Q. Colour of hair?
> A. Brown.
> Q. Is he clever?
> A. He has misled a lot of folk.
>
> Now supposing Robin Hood had concluded such question-and-answering like this: "And I'm the man." What would be added by this claim that "It is I"? There are two possible answers. Some might say, as I have admitted, that "I" is purely indicative. It just says: What you see now, this body, this chap talking with you, is of a part with all we have been describing. Nor can this be denied. The leading question is: Is that all? For another answer is possible. When Robin makes his confession, there might be a disclosure. The sequence to date, plus the pattern before the Tinker, then becomes part of a disclosure situation where the Tinker discerns around "Robin Hood" an objective challenge.[20]

Here again one can see the basic disclosure-pattern involved in personal knowledge. Clearly, the facts which are freely given by Robin while incognito are of real importance for a knowledge of Robin Hood. Nonetheless, they are given a new "depth" when experientially related to the one additional statement, "It is I!" In Ramsey's oft-used phrase, "the light dawns, the penny drops," and a whole new perspective is revealed. This type of situation takes place quite frequently within the framework of intimate friendships as well. Our knowledge of close friends and loved ones is related to, but is more than the sum of, our observations of their behavior. In fact, it is often the case that our knowledge of them as persons makes it possible for us to observe and understand certain aspects of their behavior more adequately. In Ramsey's words:

> When such a disclosure occurs around a human pattern we speak of knowing people as they "really are," of there being "deep" affection between us, of loving them "for them-selves". . . . "Husband," "mother," "father," "friend"—these are words which while they are undoubtedly associated with certain characteristic behavior patterns have a transcendent reference as well—and are grounded in disclosures.[21]

Having laid the groundwork for understanding the con-cept of disclosure by means of the foregoing examples, it is time to consider the concept of religious disclosure proper. Ramsey often uses the term "cosmic disclosure" in his discussion of this sort of experience. It is absolutely essen-tial to be perfectly clear at the outset about the one most important characteristic of religious, or cosmic, disclosure. Even as the disclosures discussed above are always medi-ated through empirical situations, religious disclosures are always so mediated as well. Moreover, and this is equally as important, one must view religious disclosures as mediated through the above-mentioned disclosures themselves! That is to say, disclosures of what may be called "the divine dimension" do not occur in an experiential vacuum, but rather arise out of perceptual, conceptual, moral, and personal disclosures, which in turn arise out of empirical settings:

> It is, I hope, evident that on this view when we appeal to "cosmic disclosures" we are not just talking about ourselves,

nor merely of our own "experience", we are not just appealing
to our own private way of looking at the world. . . . On the
contrary a cosmic disclosure reveals something of whose existence we are aware precisely because we are aware of *being*
confronted. Indeed we speak of a disclosure precisely when we
acknowledge such a confrontation, something declaring itself
to us, something relatively active when we are relatively passive.[22]

It is in this way, then, that one best understands what
has been traditionally classified as religious experience.
When one speaks of experiencing God, he is calling attention to a discernment in which there has been disclosed to
him a cosmic dimension of reality by means of the more
common disclosures arising out of experiential situations.
A person's awareness of God is similar to his awareness of
objects (as opposed to "sense data"), moral obligation, and
persons (including himself). All of this, of course, is not to
say that the claimed awareness of God is as common as
these other awarenesses, nor that it is necessarily a verid-
ical experience. What has been discussed up to this point
is the "empirical fact-and-more" nature of natural and
religious disclosure. Religious experience is seen to be
continuous with certain important aspects of everyday
experience, when the latter are understood in terms of
their disclosure nature.

Although this is not the place to delve into a consideration of theology proper, a word should be said about the
distinction most religious people draw between their
awareness of the religious dimension and their relation to a
divine being. Becoming aware of the religious dimension is
not to be equated with becoming aware of God. Perhaps
the crux of the distinction is that it is within his awareness
of the former that the theist discerns an aspect or focal
point to which only the concept of a personal being can
come close to doing justice. This is especially true in the
case of the Christian theist, who finds a corresponding
focal point in the person of Jesus. The focal point occurs
within the broader awareness of religious awareness.

One more very important aspect of this interpretation

of religious experience remains to be discussed. In every disclosure situation, on whatever level of experience, there is an element of "commitment." That is to say, whenever a disclosure "dawns" it gives rise to a corresponding commitment to act in a way which is appropriate to that which is being disclosed. In fact, it is possible to say that such commitment is what distinguishes a disclosure-situation from one which is routine or "flat." Thus it is through people's actions that their commitments are known, and through their commitments that their disclosures are known.

The universality of this element of commitment in all disclosure-situations can be seen by re-examining briefly the examples of disclosure already discussed. The grasping and using of words, sentences, and class-terms obviously involve a commitment in the sense that one's entire linguistic behavior is based upon the disclosure of this type of meaning. In this case, as in those which are to follow, it is important to avoid thinking of commitment exclusively in terms of an explicit, conscious response. Often as not, the commitments accompanying disclosures are tacit, but nonetheless real. The perception of objects and patterns also involves a tacit commitment which is appropriate to what is disclosed, as is evidenced by the fact that we navigate among pieces of furniture and master difficult skills.

As one moves up the scale of increasingly complex disclosures, the corresponding commitments become more and more explicit and conscious. Grasping concepts like "axiom," "infinite," "causation," and "probability" involves a commitment to a certain procedure in the disciplines of mathematics and science. Seeing the point of moral discourse and relating to others as persons involve disclosures which express clear-cut commitments to that which is disclosed therein, namely duty and personality. In the same way, our personal knowledge of ourselves results in a commitment, however implicit, concerning our own free activity and first person discourse. On whatever level of human experience they occur, disclosures give rise to attitudinal and behavioral commitments which are commensurate with that which is disclosed therein.

The cosmic discernment which bears religious significance also evokes a commitment appropriate to its object. Although religious commitment is similar in certain respects to that of other forms of discernment, it has its own unique characteristics as well. At the very least it is more comprehensive and carries more depth than any other commitments. Ramsey puts it this way:

> So far we have seen two kinds of discernment-commitment—"mathematical" commitment and "personal" or "quasi-personal" commitment. Religious commitment, I suggest, partakes of both. It combines the total commitment to a pastime, to a ship, to a person, with the breadth of mathematical commitment. It combines the "depth" of personal or quasi-personal loyalty—to a sport, a boat, a loved one—with the range of mathematical and scientific devotion. It is a commitment suited to the whole job of living—not one just suited to building houses, or studying inter-planetary motion, or even one suited to our own families, and no more.[23]

It is common knowledge that religious experience often brings about this high sense of commitment which, when properly interpreted, sheds light upon the totality of a person's heretofore nonreligious commitments and experiences. What is not common knowledge, and what Ramsey is concerned to point out, is that the experiential logic of religious commitment is essentially similar to that of commitments involved at other levels of experience. Such an emphasis helps in understanding both religious commitment and nonreligious commitment. The religious person's talk about God is to be understood as arising out of a disclosure-commitment situation which, in turn, both results from, and sheds light upon, the rest of his experience. Such talk will be related to object-language and will go beyond it as well.

> So our conclusion is that for the religious man "God" is a key word, an irreducible posit, an ultimate of explanation expres-

sive of the kind of *commitment* he professes. It is to be talked
about in terms of the object-language over which it presides,
but only when this object-language is qualified; in which case
this qualified object-language becomes also currency for that
odd *discernment* with which religious *commitment*, when it is
not bigotry or fanaticism, will necessarily be associated.[24]

This then is the pattern of religious experience according to Ramsey's interpretation. It remains to be said that
he associates revelation with cosmic disclosure. It should
be noted once again that this approach to revelation stands
midway between those which view it as strictly informational on the one hand, and those which view it as strictly
existential on the other. The same relationship obtains
with regard to the more extreme views of religious experience. The view discussed above does justice to both the
mystery and the empirical nature of religious experience.

With respect to the Christian religion, the historical
dimension plays an especially important role. The basic
characteristic of the Christian concept of revelation is that
God reveals himself in the events in the life of the ancient
Hebrews, and most fully in the life of Jesus and his church.
Here again the concept of cognitive experience as contextual harmonizes fruitfully with the case for the possibility of revelation by means of historic event. Within the
contexts provided by the activities of Jesus, both in their
original setting and in the biblical record, the Christian
becomes aware of a disclosure of the divine dimension to
which he responds with total commitment. Thus it is that
the historical facts and records are the necessary mediators
of religious knowledge. Revelation cannot be equated with
them, but it is impossible apart from them as well. In a
way, these factors function as catalysts for focusing religious awareness and response.

On the basis of this understanding of religious experience and revelation, it is possible to sketch the main
themes of a fresh approach to the traditional Christian
concept of miracle in general and of the resurrection of
Jesus in particular. Clearly space will not permit a discus-

sion of the philosophical pros and cons of the concept of miracle. The following points only mark a point of fresh beginning.

First, there are always certain matters of fact which, whether they are sensory or historical, serve as the empirical anchor for the discernment of a miracle. Such matters of fact relate the disclosure to public events in such a way as to guard against hallucination and fraud. Although the reality of a discernment cannot be strictly deduced from these facts, there is a sense in which they do provide some degree of verification. The objective element involved in a discernment is as real as that involved in the knowledge of other persons, although in neither case is this reality strictly deduced or inferred from empirical facts.

The second element involved in understanding the discernment of miracles is the disclosure of a dimension whose significance supersedes that of empirical facts. This is what religious people refer to as "the activity of God," and it comprises a significant aspect of what is usually termed religious experience. This disclosure is similar to becoming aware of the love and activity of a personal friend by means of his words and behavior. Third, there is the response of commitment which arises out of such a disclosure-situation. This element is clearly an essential aspect of all religious experience.

Ramsey concludes his analysis of resurrection-belief in the following fashion:

> But in emphasizing the distinctive character of the Christian belief in the Resurrection, it has been no part of my purpose to deny its essential reference to "objects of sense" as well. Indeed, on the contrary, I have tried to give a hint about how the two points can be combined, about how the logical gap can be bridged. The hint comes from recognizing what has likewise to be both distinguished and related in situations of human love and devotion. For here, too, there are "objects of sense" and more. Characteristically, personal behavior is more than "what's seen." . . . We shall be helped to meet. . .criticism if we concentrate on this personal model, and in particular if we develop the theme that while of course all personal loyalty

is anchored in some facts of an empirical kind, personal devotion never builds on empirical fact with a nicely calculated less or more.[25]

One final point needs to be made before this discussion of the contextual, awareness-response nature of religious knowledge can be brought to a close. As was indicated in some detail at the close of Chapter Five, it is the interaction between the awareness and response continua which gives rise to human knowledge. It is in this way that claims to religious knowledge are to be understood as well. As in the case of knowledge in general, religious knowledge may take a variety of forms along the continuum between the tacit and explicit poles. When one is focally aware of the religious dimension and responds conceptually, then religious knowledge is explicit. When, on the other hand, one is subsidiarily aware of, and makes a more bodily response to, the religious dimension, then religious knowledge is tacit.

Although throughout this and previous chapters it has been necessary to speak of the two interacting continua of awareness and response singly, it should be borne in mind that the relationship between them is not one of sequence. That is, a person does not usually become aware of a dimension or context and *then* respond to it. Although this is a convenient way of speaking, and harmless if not carried too far, the whole drive of Part Two of this book has been to establish the simultaneous interaction between the two continua within the various contexts and dimensions of existence. There is a sense in which one does not become aware of certain realities until he responds in certain ways. The dynamic and contextual structure of cognitive experience cannot be subjected to a more thorough analysis in terms of "the given" and the response. Awareness and activity occur simultaneously. Together they give rise to knowledge. The intricacies of the relation between these two aspects of the knowing situation cannot be made explicit. Nevertheless, they can be known tacitly since they lie at the base of the very possibility of all other knowledge.

The foregoing considerations make it necessary to conclude that, at least for the most part, religious knowledge is tacit. This follows first from the fact that the awareness of the religious dimension is always mediated by means of two other dimensions. This is why, both in traditional and contemporary theology, there is always a certain emphasis on the "hiddenness of God." To come at the point from the other side, religious knowledge is primarily tacit because the deepest religious response is always a matter of action as distinguished from concepts. This is not to suggest that the two can ever be separated from one another. It is to suggest that the more profoundly something affects us, the less adequate is our attempt to conceptualize it.

Thus out of the interaction of a subsidiary awareness of God with an indwelling response to God arises the tacit knowledge which forms the foundation of all religious knowledge. There are, to be sure, degrees to which certain aspects of tacit religious knowledge can be rendered more or less explicit. Indeed, such rendering is necessary because man is a linguistic being. Nevertheless, the most essential aspects can never be made explicit. The structure and function of efforts to render religious knowledge linguistically as explicit as possible will be treated in the next chapter.

3. THE CONFIRMATION OF RELIGIOUS KNOWLEDGE

Before considering the nature of theological language, we must deal with the question of confirming religious knowledge. The basis for dealing with this question was set forth in Section Two of Chapter Six, where it was argued that truth is a function of the purpose and setting for which and within which a given utterance is made. In this broad sense, truth is determined pragmatically. Moreover, in that section I maintained that as the cognitive context shifts from the more explicit end of the knowledge continuum to the more tacit end, the criteria for judging truth also become increasingly tacit. As these criteria become increasingly tacit, they become more a function of pragmatic indwelling than of analytic conceptualizing. Thus the truth of a tacit claim to knowledge can be adjudicated only by tracing the overall harmony and fruitfulness of the claim as it is embodied in the behavior and linguistic posits of the person making the claim.

It is on this basis, then, that the criteria for judging claims to religious knowledge must be understood. There are, to be sure, certain standard (although not absolute) criteria for judging certain explicit claims. Historical, sociological, and psychological statements often form part of one's claim to religious knowledge, and these are to be treated in the same way as other such statements and claims. However, as this explicit talk begins to shade off into more properly theological discourse, the situation becomes more tricky. Here the explicit and tacit factors become inextricably mixed and must be dealt with simultaneously. Finally, when the claims to religious knowledge operate entirely beneath the threshold of explicit knowledge, then they can be judged only in terms of activity and styles of life. Nonetheless, it is possible to evaluate such claims in terms of their overall consistency and fruitfulness.

The approach to the criteria of religious truth which I am here defending is in large measure based upon the insights of Max Black, as discussed at the close of Chapter Six. Black calls attention to the necessity of viewing the "models" upon which theoretical frameworks are built as cognitive in nature. Although more will be said in the next chapter about the model-nature of theological discourse, something needs to be said at this point in order to adequately explain the nature of religious confirmation.

Following Black and others, it must be realized that high-level models in both physical and social science are "analogue models" and not "picture models." By this I mean that such models do not simply represent the parts of a certain aspect of reality, like a model ship or cell. Rather, they integrate and illuminate the functional and structural relationships between the parts and the whole, and between the particular aspect of reality in question and human experience. Thus they are closer to metaphor in nature than they are to exact pictures. The confirmation of this type of model is not based on a one-to-one correspondence between its elements and those of an external reality. The analogue model is confirmed or disconfirmed in terms of its ability to organize, integrate, and illuminate past and present experience, and to predict and suggest new possibilities in future experience. Such confirmation is pragmatic and experiential, but is also extremely complex and flexible. In addition, there will always remain a certain element of mystery and uncertainty. The purpose of making this point is to underline the fact that the theoretical sciences are not as straightforwardly "empirical" as many empiricists maintain.

Like the high-level models of science, the models of theological discourse are also analogical. Moreover, since they are meant to help us map the complex mysteries of personal and ultimate reality, they will of necessity be even more complex and flexible than those of the theoretical sciences. Nevertheless, they are still based upon, and must be confirmed by, human experience. Every model must be scrutinized not in terms of its ability to make strict, deductive predictions about carefully controlled experiments, but in terms of its broad "empirical fit" with the facts of every area of human experience. As Ramsey puts it:

> These will be the models whose links with observable facts are not predictive, after the fashion of scientific models. These models will work in terms of what in the first lecture I called empirical fit. For it is empirical fit, rather than deductive verifications, which characterizes models which are distinctively personal. Let me illustrate. From "a loves b" nothing can be rigorously deduced which permits of appeal to experi-

ment and consequent verification or falsification. For instance, someone might allege that if "a loves b" there will be some occasion when a will be found planning for b's happiness; but a might some day plan for b's happiness simply in the hope of favours to come—and apparent experimental verification would be wholly deceptive. Alternatively, from "a loves b" someone might suppose that a would never be seen for example in any sort of way which might cause b even momentary unhappiness. But this would be a far too shallow view of human relationships; love indeed is "deepened" through tensions lived through and redeemed. In brief, "a loves b" will only be verified in terms of what I called in the last lecture "empirical fit" and the test will be how stable the assertion is as an overall characterization of a complex, multi-varied pattern of behaviour which it is impossible in a particular case to specify deductively beforehand.[26]

The criterion of religious truth, then, especially of that truth in its more tacit forms, is the criterion of empirical fit. This is about all that can be said about confirming claims to religious knowledge. Each person must look to his own experience and seek to do justice to it in the most responsible way possible. Because of the necessarily tacit roots of religious knowledge, the degree of agreement will never be as great as that in other areas of knowledge. Nevertheless, there will be, and indeed there always has been, much more agreement than many thinkers have been willing to admit. There is a large amount of "intersubjectivity" achieved among those within various religious traditions. Although it is very difficult, judgments can be made and are made concerning claims to religious knowledge. There is a difference between a person who believes certain religious claims for all the wrong reasons (because his parents did, because it's comforting, etc.) and the person who believes as a result of profound existential struggle and honest cognitive searching. This difference is best accounted for in terms of the concept of religious knowledge as tacit.

One final facet of the nature of religious confirmation needs to be emphasized. As I have maintained all along, the more tacit the knowledge the more it is expressed in terms of active embodiment or indwelling. This is especially true of religious knowledge. Thus the more appropriate criterion for evaluating claims to religious knowledge is that of the quality of life embodied in the claim. In other words, there is a sense in which only by participating in, or indwelling, the religious way of life can a person come to know the force and value of its claims. This is, of course, true of any other "form of life" as well. Only to the degree that one participates in such realities as friendship, marriage, democracy, and scientific or philosophic activity will he be able to ascertain the value of the knowledge that pertains to them. In the final analysis all knowledge is based upon commitment. In the words of my former colleague, Carl F. Walters:

> There may be some questions which are not adequately answered merely by continued speculation and discussion. Some knowledge is not available to us simply through abstract conception and oral or written language. Although we may have technical knowledge of the factual data of tone, timing, and rhythm pattern, we may not *know* Handel's *Messiah* in the fullest sense until we give ourselves to it and take a part in singing it. Similarly, we cannot say that we truly dig James Brown's music until we let ourselves go and dance to it. You will not really know your wife or husband (if ever) until you embrace her or him in committed, responsible, and vulnerable love. In analogous fashion, we may not really know the God of Jesus until we identify with him and participate in his self-giving, life-giving action—wherever it is. Even then the elements of uncertainty and risk, the possibility of doubt, and the necessity of faith, will not be excluded.[27]

Part One of the present work was devoted to an analysis of the contemporary stalemate between empiricism and existentialism resulting from their mutual acceptance of the fact-value dichotomy. In particular, this epistemological dualism was seen to lie at the heart of the difficulty over the possibility of religious knowledge. In short, if the knowledge of God is related to the factual realm too exclusively it is impossible for it to meet the requirements for cognitivity; if it is related to the valuational realm too exclusively it loses its cognitive significance. Part Two of the present work was devoted to replacing the contemporary dichotomy between fact and value with a view of language and knowledge based upon dimensional and contextual significance. In this way knowledge was seen to be a continuum stretched between the tacit and explicit poles, which in turn are the function of the interaction between awareness and response.

In particular, this contextual epistemology, and especially its concept of tacit knowledge, has provided a way of approaching the possibility of religious knowledge in a more fruitful way. In this chapter I have argued on behalf of this possibility by suggesting the following: 1) that religious experience be understood as a mediated awareness of a religious dimension; 2) that revelation be viewed as mediated by means of the other dimensions of experience; 3) that religious knowledge be interpreted as primarily tacit in structure; 4) that religious truth be ascertained as a function of the relation between the claim and the total context in which it is made. An understanding of knowledge as tacit combines the factual and valuational dimensions in such a way as to make the concept of religious knowledge a viable possibility.

VIII: Theological Language: Metaphors and Models

Assuming the adequacy of the epistemological reconstruction presented in the foregoing chapters, what then is to be said about theology? What is its purpose and what should be its method? I believe that the position argued for up to this point implies that theology must be viewed as the attempt to conceptualize in a systematic way the insights obtained by religious knowledge. In essence this becomes a task of charting and regulating religious language in general and God-talk in particular, since it is by means of such talk that religious persons seek to communicate about their common experience. In short, theology is essentially a linguistic activity. Its purpose is to lay bare the main themes of religious knowledge as they are embodied in our language. Its method is the analysis and regulation of religious language. Thus theological language is a "meta," or second-level, linguistic activity.

In this final chapter I will attempt to sketch the broad outlines of the basic structure of theological language. The first section will provide some foundational material on the logical status of metaphorical and paradoxical language. The second section will be devoted to mapping the two-dimensional structure of language which seeks to speak about God. The final section will focus specifically on the logic of the term "God" itself. In this way the positive goal of the present book will, I hope, have been reached. At least the linguistic emphasis will have come full circle from the beginning of Part Two, where a fresh approach to language was presented.

1. THE STATUS OF "ODD-TALK"

In Chapter Four the early Wittgenstein was quoted as maintaining that "What can be said at all can be said clearly, and what we cannot talk about we must consign to silence." This statement clearly summarizes the position against which I have been arguing all along. The work of such thinkers as the later Wittgenstein, J. L. Austin, and Michael Polanyi would suggest turning the above motto inside-out so as to make it read more like the following: "Not everything that can be said can be said clearly, and what we cannot remain silent about we must speak of as best we can." This statement will serve as the motto for the present consideration of the structure of theological language.

Since theological language is admittedly "odd" in relation to the language of science or mathematics, it will be helpful to begin by considering the logical status of "odd-talk" in general. As is well known, the influence of logical empiricism has rendered suspect all discourse which is not scientifically oriented. The verifiability theory of meaning has eliminated from the realm of meaningful discourse all but straightforwardly empirical locutions. It should not be thought that this emphasis on establishing workable criteria for determining cognitive significance has had only negative results. Clearly such criteria are needed, and the influence of logical empiricism has brought this need to the fore. The shortcomings of this influence derive from the overly narrow conception of cognitive experience upon which logical empiricism is based. The shortcomings of the existentialist influence, on the other hand, derive from an overly vague conception of cognitive experience.

As I argued in some detail in Chapter Four, the narrow conception of cognitive experience upon which logical empiricism is based results from a limited view of the function of language. What ultimately underlies the suspicion with which contemporary empiricism views all seemingly odd language is the assumption that the sole cognitive function of language is the representation, or "picturing," of matters of fact. Given this assumption, it is clear that all odd language, including theological language, must be dismissed as cognitively useless. The case against granting this assumption, together with a more adequate and realistic interpretation of the function of language and the structure of cognitive experience, has already been presented.

The later work of Wittgenstein and the work of J. L. Austin have served to break the trail toward a more sympathetic understanding of language that displays a nonconformist structure. Wittgenstein argued both for a greater tolerance with respect to meaningfulness, and for a more flexible view of cognitivity in language. Austin stressed the importance of seeing language as an activity involving many simultaneous forces which cannot be isolated from one another. Max Black, in turn, has contributed to this broader view of nonconformist language by arguing for the cognitivity of discourse based upon metaphors and models. Here, then, is the seed for the development of a view of the logical status of odd-talk which opens up a more adequate interpretation of talk about God.

One thinker who has made a most direct application of these insights is John Wisdom. In *Paradox and Discovery* there are four main themes bearing directly on the question of the status of talk which seems at first odd. The overall thesis of Wisdom's position is that odd-talk is frequently necessary, both as a means to communicate and as a means to discover truth. Although he does not argue for the wholesale acceptance of all odd-talk, Wisdom does argue for a sympathetic and exploratory approach to all such talk. Moreover, he maintains that odd-talk is not limited to nonscientific discourse. "I am urging that there is more of poetry in science and more of science in poetry than our philosophy permits us readily to grasp."[1]

The first theme in Wisdom's book pertains to the nature of metaphorical language. Along with Max Black, Wisdom maintains that far from being odd or dispensable, metaphorical language is very common and essential to the cognitive function of language in general. He focuses on the concrete case of a woman finally deciding not to purchase a hat because while she was trying to make up her mind a friend said, "My dear, it's the Taj Mahal." Against those who would argue that such a statement only influences the hearer's noncognitive feelings about the hat and can be reduced to statements about the hat being "like" the Taj Mahal, Wisdom says:

> My answer is this: In the first place it isn't true that the words about the hat only influence the hearer's feelings to the hat. They alter her apprehension of the hat just as the word "A hare" makes what did look like a clump of earth *look* like an animal, a hare in fact; just as the word "A cobra" may change the look of something in the corner by the bed. It is just because in these instances words change the apprehension of what is already before one that I refer to them.
>   Again it isn't true that the words "It's the Taj Mahal" meant "It is like the Taj Mahal." This more sober phrase is an inadequate substitute. This reformulation is a failure. It's feebler than the original and yet it's still too strong. For the hat isn't like the Taj Mahal, it's much smaller and the shape is very different. And the still more sober substitute "It is in some respects like the Taj Mahal" is still more inadequate. It's *much* too feeble. Everything is like everything in some respects—a man like a monkey, a monkey like a mongoose, a mongoose like a mouse, a mouse like a micro-organism, and a man after all is an organism too. Heaven forbid that we should say there are no contexts in which it is worth while to remark this sort of thing. But it is not what the woman in the hat shop remarked. What she said wasn't the literal truth like "It's a cobra" said of what is, unfortunately, a cobra. But what she said revealed the truth.[2]

This tendency to dismiss odd-talk as meaningless is even stronger with respect to paradoxical language than it is with respect to metaphorical language. The relation between paradox and truth is the second of Wisdom's major themes. Wisdom maintains that paradoxical language often leads to a new and deeper understanding of experience and reality. Perhaps the most extreme case of a paradoxical use of language (as distinguished from a paradoxical statement) is irony. When a statement is made ironically its meaning is in direct contradiction with what is said. To use Austin's terms, its illocutionary force is at odds with its locutionary force. In irony the speaker says the exact opposite of what he means—yet he expects his meaning to be understood! Not only is the ironic use of language paradoxical, but the language used to talk about its paradoxical nature is also paradoxical. Witness the above perfectly understandable statement that in irony one says the opposite of what he means.

Wisdom traces the empiricist's nervousness in the face of paradoxical language to two sources. One is simply the failure to comprehend the point that is being made by such language, and this may in turn be based on a legitimate intellectual difficulty. Another source is the concern to avoid being victimized by misleading or meaningless confusion. Although he agrees that a good deal of caution and rational analysis is always in order, Wisdom also maintains that

> Such fear, such obsessional fear, of any concept which begins to be not quite itself may indeed join with inadequate comprehension of such eccentricity to cramp our power to conceive the conceivable. For it is with words mainly that we delineate the conceivable and if we never allow words to be a little eccentric, never allow ourselves to apply a word to any state of affairs actual or conceivable, to which it would not customarily be applied, we are without means to refer to any state of affairs for which there is not yet a word, any possibility undreamt of in our philosophy.[3]

Wisdom's third theme presents itself in his attitude towards metaphysical language. He thinks that a healthy respect for metaphor and paradox should render one much less critical of the sort of thing metaphysically inclined philosophers are prone to say. There is, of course, an important distinction to be drawn between what metaphysicians say when they are *doing* their work and what they may say *about* what they are doing. This is an important distinction with respect to any discipline. The practitioner is often the least reliable theoretician, in science and mathematics as well as in art. Space will not permit a detailed account of Wisdom's analysis of the function of metaphysical discourse, but the following quotation should point up the core of his approach:

> I believe that if, faced with the extraordinary pronouncements of metaphysicians, we avoid asking them to define their terms, but instead press them to present us with instances of what they refer to contrasted with instances of what they do not refer to, then their pronouncements will no longer appear either as obvious falsehoods or mysterious truths or pretentious nonsense, but as often confusingly presented attempts to bring before our attention certain not fully recognized and yet familiar features of how in the end questions of different types are met.[4]

On the basis of the foregoing emphasis, Wisdom suggests, as yet a fourth theme, that theological discourse can be recalled from the exile to which it was banished by overly eager empiricist philosophers. Once again it must be stressed that such a view does not imply the acceptance of every religious or theological statement as meaningful. It simply implies that each such statement must be dealt with individually within the immediate and broader context wherein it occurs. Wisdom puts it emphatically:

> One might have expected that in the sphere of religion everyone would have learned by now to move carefully and neither at once to accept nor hastily to reject what sounds bewildering. But no, even here we still find a tendency to reject strange statements with impatience, to turn from them as absurd or unprovable or to write them down as metaphor—deceptive or at best merely picturesque. Only a few months ago someone came to me troubled about the old but bewildering statement that Christ was both God and man. He had asked those who taught him theology how this *could* be true. Their answers had not satisfied him. I was not able to tell him what the doctrine means. But I did remind him that though some statements which seem self-contradictory are self-contradictory others are

> not, that indeed some of the most preposterous statements
> ever made have turned out to convey the most tremendous
> discoveries.[5]

This same theme is developed in Wisdom's famous paper on "Gods,"[6] where he maintains that the logic of the question of God's existence lies somewhere between that of empirical questions and nonempirical questions. He concludes that the sort of reasoning involved in theological questions is most like that employed in judging a legal case or a work of art, in which the factual and valuational dimensions are blended.

The foregoing considerations provide the overture for the detailed analysis of theological language which is to follow. I have argued that odd-talk needs to be explored rather than rejected out of hand. Metaphor, paradox, and metaphysics are as necessary to the cognitive enterprise as they are difficult to interpret. It is time to switch the focus of the present chapter from odd-talk in general to God-talk in particular.

2. SPEAKING OF GOD: MODELS AND QUALIFIERS

Cognitive experience in general and religious experience in particular have been seen to have a multi-dimensional structure. Within any given context, a person's awareness of various levels of reality is best understood as an awareness of a higher, more inclusive dimension which is mediated by means of the other, less inclusive dimensions. Moreover, a person's response within any such context is also mediated in the sense that it is directed toward the higher dimension by means of the lower dimensions. Not only is religious awareness mediated through physical and moral awareness, but religious commitment is mediated through or expressed in terms of these other awarenesses as well.

In the light of this situation it is to be expected that discourse seeking to communicate about dimensions which can be known only by mediation will reflect a seemingly odd logical structure. Language arising in a mediated and partially tacit cognitive context will necessarily take on a highly "refracted" or complicated structure. Only in this way can it do justice to the complexity of the dimension of experience within which it arises. Theological language is especially complex because it is twice removed, because it is uttered in response to a doubly mediated experiential dimension.

Since religious awareness is mediated by means of other, more common forms of cognitive awareness, it is only natural that the structure of religious and theological language should be two-fold. On the one hand, such language uses terms and expressions borrowed directly from other, less mediated dimensions of experience and language-games. This aspect of the structure of theological language corresponds to the fact that awareness of the religious dimension is always mediated and never direct or isolated. On the other hand, the use of these terms borrowed from the more common language-games never follows the usual pattern. This aspect of theological language corresponds to the fact that awareness of the religious dimension is never reducible to, nor accounted for in terms of, the other awareness through which it is mediated.

Another way to put this point is this. Just as in religious knowledge one is aware of an aspect of reality which discloses itself by means of other aspects without being equatable with them, so in theological language one speaks of this aspect of reality in terms of these other aspects, but in a qualified sense. Apart from common language, theological discourse could not exist, since the mediated character of religious awareness eliminates the possibility of both a direct experience of the divine and a language uniquely appropriate to it. However, apart from some form of qualification accompanying the use of common language, theological discourse would also be impossible, since there would be no way to acknowledge the transcendent aspect of religious awareness. Thus theological language must exhibit a two-fold structure in order to meet the standards of meaningfulness and transcendence.

No one else has analyzed the two-fold structure of theological language as thoroughly as has Dr. Ramsey, who has carefully scrutinized traditional theological locutions and biblical language in an effort to trace their two-dimensional logic. Ramsey classifies the traditional characterizations of God according to three kinds: 1) the attributes of negative theology; 2) the one-word attributes of positive characterization; and 3) the two-word attributes of positive characterization. The following discussion will draw heavily upon Ramsey's insights.

By negative attributes Ramsey is referring to that aspect of religious experience which does not participate in the fluctuation of everyday experience, but which, rather, is the very thing which holds the changing aspects of experience together as a unity. In other words, a negative characterization of God, such as "God is immutable," is an attempt to call attention to that aspect of religious experience which provides the continuity or structure of any and all experience. Obviously, it is difficult, if not impossible, to give positive labels to this element of experience which one has discerned. This is the reason why characterizations of such discernments take a negative, and thus logically odd, form.

Perhaps the most illuminating illustration Ramsey gives of this type of discernment is in his analysis of what occurs when one is confronted with an old friend whom he has not seen for many years. Clearly much, if not most, has changed. Yet not everything has changed, and it is this discernment which causes one to say, for example, "He is still the same," or "He hasn't really changed." It is in this way that negative descriptions of God function as symbols of that which has been discerned as unchanging in our experience. In addition the main function of using such terms is not to describe God scientifically, but to evoke a situation in which one will be able to discern this peculiar aspect of experience. Ramsey summarizes the point in this way:

> So when we talk of God as "immutable," or as "impassible," the function of these particular attribute-words is primarily to evoke the kind of situation we have just been mentioning; to fix on mutable and passible features of perceptual situations and to develop these features in such a way that there is evoked a characteristically different situation which is the foundation *in fact* for assertions about God's immutability or impassibility. But there is a little more to it than that. For these words "immutability" and "impassibility" make also a *language* plea. They claim for the word "God" a position outside all mutable and passible language. Beyond that negative claim the attributes of negative theology do not however go. All they tell us is that if anything is "mutable" it will not be exact currency for God; and if anything is "passible" it will not be exact currency for God. So the main merit of attribute words like "immutable" and "impassible" is to give a kind of technique for meditation; their main merit is evocative.[7]

Positive characterizations of God that make use of only one word can best be understood as attempts to describe God by means of contrast. The term "unity," for example, is used to call attention to the discernment that often arises out of an exposure to the diversity of experience. Such is the case in the understanding and use of class, or set, theory, and also in the experiences evoked by experiments in Gestalt psychology.

The terms "simplicity" and "perfection" applied to God represent the same attempt at characterization by contrast. The latter term is of special interest because of its importance throughout the history of philosophical and religious thought. One learns the use of terms like "perfection" by inductively examining various imperfect aspects of experience, and ordering them according to their decreasing imperfection until "the penny drops" and one discerns what is meant. Such terms do not point to some unseen, Platonic form, nor to a mental picture. Nonetheless, the experience of learning how to use such terms involves a discernment of some aspect of experience which is nonetheless real for being mental. This type of characterization of God suggests that "perfection" functions in a way very similar to the concept of a limit in mathematics.

The last kind of characterization, that which makes a two-word positive predication about God, does the most to illuminate both the empirical ground and logical oddity of religious language. Ramsey deals with five examples: "first cause," "infinitely wise," "infinitely good," "creation out of nothing," and "eternal purpose."[8]

The pattern of such terms is two-fold. First, in the words "cause," "wise," "good," "creation," "purpose," and others like them, we have a "model." That is, a term is used to designate a situation with which people are generally acquainted in experience. It brings to mind examples of causal relations, wise people, good people, making things, human purposes, and the like. A model thus serves to anchor these theological phrases in experience.

Second, in the words "first," "infinite," "out-of-nothing," and "eternal" we have what Ramsey calls a "qualifier." This "qualifier" has at least two separate functions, namely, 1) to indicate in which direction the models are to be developed, and 2) to express the logical priority of the model term when used in connection with God. The function of indicating the direction in which to develop a particular model has to do with suggesting that, when used in discourse about God, words like "cause," "wise," and "good" are to be developed in the direction of their higher degrees. This would seem to be a type of "analogical pointer" in that one is saying "Begin here and move in that direction." Such a "pointer" is not to be mistaken for a description of the destination.

The function of expressing the logical priority of model terms is similar to that of terms like "infinite" in conjunction with "sum" in the language of mathematics. Although the phrase "infinite sum" may have the same grammar as such phrases as "large sum" and "small sum," it has a distinctively different logic. Similarly, such phrases as "infinitely good" and "eternal purpose" have the same grammar as "very good" and "long-range purpose" respectively, but their logic is very different.

In no sense are the characterizations of God in religious language to be taken as metaphysical or psychological descriptions. These characterizations are much more akin to the language of metaphor and parable, which, incidentally, pervades even our mathematical and scientific language, to say nothing of ordinary discourse. When one discerns a new relationship, in any area of experience, which does not quite fit into previous categories, new words are coined, or words are borrowed from other areas of experience, in order to express this new "disclosure." These new or borrowed words often take on a logic of their own. Much confusion has resulted from the failure of theologians and philosophers to pay sufficient attention to the logical oddness of religious characterizations of God.

Perhaps the value of this interpretation of talk about God as having a two-fold logic can be made clear if we apply it to several key New Testament phrases. First, consider the phrase "eternal life" (John 17:3). This phrase is very often construed to have reference only to the quantity of life. Moreover, it is often thought of as something that begins when this earthly life is over. Both of these interpretations fail to come to grips with much of the significance of the concept. A study of the contexts in which the phrase "eternal life" is found indicates that it has a very definite qualitative connotation as well as a quantitative one. "Life" (zōē) serves as a model, or empirical anchor, while "eternal" (aiōnios) serves as a logical qualifier. The former term suggests a similarity between Christian experience and natural, everyday life. To the one looking for an understanding of Christian experience it says, "Begin with the experience of living, as opposed to being inanimate." The term "eternal" on the other hand, suggests a basic, logical dissimilarity between Christian experience and natural, everyday life. To the inquirer it says, "Develop your concept along the lines of higher qualities of life—'eternal' signifies the highest possible."

Second, consider "living water" (John 4:10ff.). Here Jesus is attempting to communicate with an individual person in a specific situation. For this reason this phrase is of special significance for ascertaining the meaning of religious language. "Living water" clearly fits the pattern suggested, with "living" serving as a logical qualifier of the model, "water." Once again we see one part of the term grounding itself in experience, while the other part points out the direction in which one ought to move in an effort to discern both the significance and the mystery of that which is being discussed.

Two more examples from the language of Jesus. In another concrete situation with an individual person, Jesus said that a man must be "born anew" (or "from above," John 3:3). Once more the model ("born") and qualifier ("anew," or "from above") pattern can be seen. In other words, the Christian experience is similar to the birth experience, only it is of a logically different order. Clearly the phrase "from above" is not meant as a literal description. Rather it symbolizes the qualitative significance of the Christian experience. In this same passage, and elsewhere, the phrase "kingdom of God" is used by Jesus, and it too can be said to follow this basic pattern.

Finally, consider the phrase "Heavenly Father" (or often just "the Father"). "Father" serves as a starting point in experience (a model) for those who were listening to Jesus talk, and "Heavenly" (or "the") serves as a warning sign (a qualifier) that there is a logical difference between this statement and the more familiar statements about fathers, such as "old father" and "nice father." Such a statement shows one where to begin, with progenitors, and in which direction to move, toward increasingly higher forms of progenitors, until the "penny drops" and one discerns what is meant.

Ramsey pointedly summarizes the contention of this section when he says:

Christian doctrine does not give a picture of God in the sense
of a verbal photograph. Christian doctrine can only be justified
on an epistemology very different from that which lay behind
traditional views of metaphysics. In no sense is Christian
doctrine a "super science." Its structure, and its anchorage in
"fact" are much more complex than that parallel would suggest. What we have been trying to do in these various examples
has been to give hints—no more—of how traditional Christian
phrases might otherwise be elucidated and justified. If they are
anchored in "disclosure" situations, situations which centre
directly or indirectly on Jesus of Nazareth and are in part
mysterious and elusive, only then can Christian phrases be
given a logical complexity suited to their theme. An empirical
approach to philosophical theology takes the traditional
phrases of Christian doctrine and sees in this way what logical
placing they must have to tell their tale; being sure of only one
thing, that an adequate account of their logical structure will
never be given on an ordinary view of "facts" accompanied by
the idea that language provides a sort of verbal photograph
which is in a one-one correspondence to what it talks about.
To make such a mistake would be to confound the logic of
theology with that of some precision language such as those of
which the sciences make use.[9]

The foregoing exploration of Ramsey's analysis of talk
about God is aimed at establishing two conclusions. First,
it substantiates the contention that theological language,
like other forms of odd-talk, can be interpreted as having
cognitive meaning if it is approached with a careful and
sympathetic eye. Second, it substantiates the claim that
theological language exhibits a logical structure which ap-
propriately corresponds to the mediational structure of
cognitive experience in general and of religious knowledge
in particular. It is in this way that the main themes of the
present chapter harmonize with those of the preceding
chapters. The contextual and mediated structures of cognitive experience, together with the tacit and functional view
of religious knowledge, give rise to a metaphorical and
analogical interpretation of theological language. More
specifically, the parallels between the concept of qualified
models and Black's "interaction" view of metaphor are
quite plain. The main perspective underlying the explora-

tion of this section is clearly that of Wittgenstein and Austin. Theological language has been examined with reference to its use in context, and with respect to its simultaneous forces.

One important corollary following from the above interpretation of theological discourse warrants special mention. It pertains to the nature of theological activity in general. The approximate and flexible character of theological language serves to underline the fact that theology is, after all, a human enterprise. Although this may sound like a truism, it is at least one truism which bears repeating. Being a human enterprise not only means that theology is fallible, but also means that theology is in constant need of updating in order to insure its accuracy and relevance. In sum, theology must always be viewed as flexible and tentative in nature. Such tentativeness does not imply that religious knowledge is entirely relative or subjective. It implies only that theological endeavor must always be self-critical and open to better insights. Far from placing theology in an uneasy position, such a view provides the only assurance against theological bigotry and for increased religious knowledge.

Perhaps it will facilitate understanding if I conclude this section by stating this point in terms of the distinction between tacit and explicit knowledge. Theology should be viewed as the effort to become as explicit as possible about that dimension of experience which gives rise to religious awareness and knowledge. Due, however, to the double-mediated structure of such awareness, there is much that is known religiously that cannot be made explicit. In short, theology lives on the threshold between the tacit and the explicit. It seeks to chart the mystery of the tacit as clearly as possible, while acknowledging the necessary incompleteness of such charting. Whereof one cannot remain silent, thereof one must speak as best he can: by means of metaphors and models.

3. GOD-TALK AND I-TALK

Having discussed the ways in which odd-talk in general and God-talk in particular can be understood as possessing cognitive meaning, we must now say something about the logic of the term "God" itself. Talk about God can be understood in terms of qualified models and metaphors, but this approach will not cast much light on the term "God." This term is not, after all, either a model or a metaphor. In fact, "God" seems to function as a proper name, although it is not properly the name of a "person, place, or thing." Just what is its logic?

I submit that the most helpful parallel for understanding the logic of "God" is the logic of "I." Here is another term which seems to function much as a proper name, without fitting the pattern exactly. As names, both "I" and "God" are somewhat odd; yet they are equally common in everyday speech. Moreover, since it is especially in the mediation provided by our dimension of self-awareness that we discern the religious dimension, there is an intimate experiential point of connection between the logics of the terms used to communicate about them. The way "I" is used to call attention to the self provides an excellent clue to the way "God" is used to call attention to the divine. In Novak's words:

> The difficulty is that just as we have no suitable language for talking about the self, so we have no suitable language for talking about God. Language borrowed from the object world is systematically misleading when applied to the self or to God. (The positivist, of course, experiences difficulties in both matters.) Nevertheless, language about God may have an empirical ground just as language about the self does; only it will have to be one step more indirect. Our awareness of our self is a criterion for the language we use about the self; by it, we can decide which predicates are more, which less, suitable for speaking of the self.[10]

It will be necessary to digress for a few pages in order to approach the question of the function of "I" in a way that will shed light on the logic of the term "God."[11] Although discussions of the nature of the self have been frequent throughout the history of philosophy, it is only with the advent of language philosophy in contemporary times that the question has been broached from the linguistic side. It is to be hoped that the contemporary discussion of the significance of "I," while illuminating the traditional theories of the self propounded by the likes of Plato, Aristotle, Descartes, Hume, and Kant, has also progressed a good distance beyond these theories.

The implications of the use of the term "I" troubled the later Wittgenstein in much the same way that the problem of the self had troubled him earlier. In the *Blue Book* Wittgenstein suggests that there are two uses of the term "I": what he calls "the object use" and "the subject use."[12] He maintains that in the object-use, "I" can be replaced by some such phrase as "this body," while in the subject-use, "I" can never be so replaced. Wittgenstein offers the statements 1) "I am happy" and 2) "I weigh 12 stone" as examples of the subject and object uses, respectively. In the latter statement the "I" can be replaced by "this body," but no such substitution will serve in the former. In "I weigh 12 stone" the speaker is making a statement *and* talking about himself as an object, while in "I am happy" the speaker is not talking about himself as an object, but is simply making the statement as the subject. Wittgenstein goes on to maintain that there is a sense in which subject-uses of "I" are superfluous, since they do not denote, or refer to, the speaker, but are part of the act of speaking. This distinction between the two uses of "I" seems to lead to what Strawson calls the "no-ownership" theory of the self.

Moving on to the *Investigations,* we find two main passages that shed additional light on Wittgenstein's worries over the use of "I." First, there are those paragraphs about "pain-talk."[13] Wittgenstein says that the "I" in "I am in pain" (subject use) does not name a person, although there may well be situations in which such a statement could be used to call attention to the speaker (object use). Most of the time, however, such a statement is used not to designate the speaker, but as part of the speaker's "pain-behavior." That is to say, in such cases the statement functions much like "ouch," or as a groan. Wittgenstein gives roughly two reasons for this interpretation of the subject use. First, for the speaker there is never any question of being mistaken; i.e. no observations are necessary to be able to make the statement, "I am in pain," as would be the case with such statements as "He is in pain." The question of being "right" or "wrong" is never at issue. Thus the term "I" in "I am in pain" does not refer to, or name, anyone; the question of identity, to say nothing of the problem of the criteria of identity, never arises. Secondly, the "I" in such uses seems to function more like "here" and "this," and although such demonstratives are connected with names, they do not themselves name.

In Part Two of the *Investigations*, Wittgenstein comes at this theme from a slightly different angle.[14] There he says that the "I" in statements of belief (such as "I believe it is Wednesday"), when they are not being used as psychological hypotheses (object use), is superfluous. His reasoning is again, roughly two-fold. First, it can be seen that nothing is lost from the meaning of the statement when the phrase "I believe" is dropped off. To say "It is Wednesday" is equivalent to saying "I believe it is Wednesday" (unless, of course, the speaker is attempting to register his hesitancy). Second, here again it is impossible for the speaker to be wrong about, or to mistrust, his own beliefs, since he does not obtain them by means of inference, etc. "If there were a verb meaning 'to believe falsely,' it would not have any significant first person present indicative."[15]

Thus after having distinguished between the subject and object use of "I," Wittgenstein seems to have concluded that the subject use does not refer, nor name, and is, hence, superfluous. Yet there seems to be an uneasiness haunting these passages, not unlike the uneasiness haunting those passages in the *Tractatus* that deal with the self and the limits of language, thought, and reality. This uneasiness reveals itself in the *Investigations* in such comments as: "My own relation to my words is wholly different from other people's."[16] Perhaps the subject use of "I" is not as superfluous as it seems! But more of this later.

Both Gilbert Ryle and P. F. Strawson have addressed themselves to Wittgenstein's distinction between the subject and object uses of "I," and its relation to the concept of self. After maintaining that self-knowledge is obtained in much the same way as knowledge of others, namely by observing behavior (especially "unstudied talk"), Ryle argues that the mystery often felt in connection with the concept of the self is due to what he terms "the systematic elusiveness of 'I'." He maintains that once the logic of the first person singular pronoun is understood, there is no longer any need to feel or talk about mystery in relation to the concept of the self.[17]

Having developed certain distinctions among the various functions of pronouns, in much the same way as did Wittgenstein, Ryle calls attention to what he calls "higher order actions." Activities or statements can be said to function independently in what they do or say. That is, they need not be viewed as having an antecedent in response to which they are done or said. In this sense they are "first-order" actions. On the other hand, activities or statements can function as responses to other activities or statements, and in this way can be said to be dependent upon them. In this case they are "second-order" actions. Now, certain types of statements, like descriptions, when made with reference to other persons function as second-order, or higher order actions. At an early stage in his development a child learns how to "play the game" of higher order actions in relation to those with whom he has to deal. At a still later stage, a child "discovers the trick of directing higher order acts upon his own lower order acts."[18]

According to Ryle, the application of this distinction

between lower and higher order actions makes two important contributions toward solving the difficulties connected with "I." First, it explains why a person cannot ex-
haustively describe himself in any given statement, since
that statement cannot describe itself. It can, however, be
encompassed by the next order statement, *ad infinitum*. In
this way nothing need, in principle, escape description.
Second, this distinction explains the logico-grammatical
differences between the pronouns "I" and "you." And all
this without recourse to any mysterious concept of the
ego! Thus, for Ryle, the systematic elusiveness of the term
"I" is explained by the concept of higher order actions,
and it, in turn, explains the seeming systematic elusiveness
of the self. Ryle concludes his discussion of the matter by
admitting that the constancy between "I" and the speaker
"seems to endow 'I' with a mystifying uniqueness and
adhesiveness."[19] He is confident, however, that such a
"besetting feeling" is not really mysterious.

In responding to certain aspects of Wittgenstein's "no-
ownership" theory, Strawson maintains that this theory is
essentially self-stultifying in that the concept of a person,
or of a self, as more than "a bundle of perceptions," is
necessary to the denial of any such entity. Witness Hume's
infamous statement: "I never can catch *myself* at any time
without a perception, and never can observe anything but
the perception." Put linguistically, this same point can be
made by saying that terms like "I," "my," and "person,"
are necessary to the denial of the existence of a self,
whether it be one's own or another's. Moreover, Strawson
continues, we do *in fact* ascribe states of consciousness to
ourselves, as well as to others.[20]

The way out of such muddles, according to Strawson, is
simply to admit that the concept of a person is a foundational part of the framework of our language, and is in this
sense "logically-primitive."[21] By thus placing the concept
of a person within the framework of our language, Strawson seeks to avoid the mistakes both of those who have
placed it within the content of experience, and of those

who have denied the possibility of placing it at all. By a
"person" Strawson means an entity such that both states
of consciousness and corporeal characteristics can be
ascribed to it. By "logically primitive" he means both that
it is necessarily prior to the concept of individual self-
consciousness, and that it is not analyzable (reducible) in
terms of either "body" or "soul."

On the basis of the logical primitiveness of the concept
of a person, Strawson concludes:

> So, then, the word "I" never refers to this, the pure subject.
> But this does not mean, as the no-ownership theorist must
> think, that "I" in some cases does not refer at all. It refers;
> because I am a person among others; and the predicates which
> would, *per impossible*, belong to the pure subject if it could be
> referred to, belong properly to the person to which "I" does
> refer.[22]

Thus by uniting what Wittgenstein had termed the "subject-use" and the "object-use" of "I" in the concept of a
person, Strawson seeks to eliminate the mystery of "I"
without eliminating its important function within our conceptual scheme.

While I find the discussions sketched above quite valuable, there still seems to me to be something, if not
mysterious, at least "odd" about the logic of "I" which
these discussions leave unconsidered. I will try to articulate
my misgivings in the following two points.

First, to analyze the logic of the term "I" in terms of
higher and lower order actions does not tell the whole
story. Ryle, and perhaps Strawson as well, tends to imply
that what Wittgenstein calls the "subject-use" of "I" is
superfluous because it can be "translated" (reduced?) into
its "object use." I think, rather, that the subject-use of "I"
serves at least two important functions in ordinary language which render it far from superfluous. To begin with,
it at least calls attention to the fact that higher order
statements are necessary, and yet systematically inadequate, when one discusses his own activities. Hopefully
this would serve as a deterrent to those who would be

tempted to strive toward a "Laplacean" description of human experience.

In addition,[23] the so-called subject-use of "I" would seem to have a function in providing for, or at least indicating the existence of, the concept of "personal identity" as one moves from lower to higher order descriptions of one's own activities. After all, the person who makes higher order statements about himself must be the same person as the one he describes in the lower order activity and he must be aware of this identity as well! This bridge of personal identity is what seems to me to be most lacking from Ryle's account. My point is simply that there is a sense in which the subject-use of "I" is a token self-reflexive, and thus provides the logical connection between the subject and object of a higher order statement about oneself. In this way "I" does function as a name.

Secondly, there are two "oddities" about the logical grammar of "I" which have not been discussed by Ryle or Strawson, and which further underline the significance of its systematic elusiveness.[24] The first oddity to be noted is that while the term "I" can be used in conjunction with the past tense of nearly all ordinary verbs, it cannot be so used with the past tense of "die." Obviously one can say "I will die," or "I am dying," but the statement "I died" has no place in our language. But further, even the statement "I will die" exhibits an oddity in the logic of "I," since when one uses this statement in a non-casual manner he is calling attention to something which is not exhausted by predictions about what will happen to his body. A speaker's statements about himself are not equivalent to statements about his body. Moreover, there is a difference between one's relationship to his statements about himself *as* he *makes* them and when he *describes* them. When one moves from a first-order action to a second-order action, not everything in the first-order action can be captured.

The second oddity to be noted is that "I," like other pronouns such as "you" and "he," and unlike proper names, is part of our language by virtue of the fact that it can be used in connection with any person whatever. However, unlike the other pronouns, "I" can mean one and only one person on any given occasion, namely, the speaker. Perhaps one way to make this point clearer is to say that when the other pronouns are used, a question can arise concerning whom the speaker means, but when "I" is used no such question can arise. Here again the reflexive, naming, or "pointing" function of "I" is displayed. Moreover, there is a sense in which the subject-use of "I" might be said to fulfill a "performative function" within the speech-act of the speaker. Beginning a statement with the subject-use of "I" might well be considered part of the act of making the statement.

The significance of noting these two oddities about the grammatical logic of "I" can best be seen in relation to Strawson's concept of logical primitiveness. There simply is something basic, or unique, or axiomatic about the relation of a speaker to his own statements, and this uniqueness is reflected in the logic of the term "I." Here is a bit of "linguistic phenomenology" which not only points up the logical "ins and outs" of certain terms, but which points up an important dimension of our conceptual framework as well.

Now I want to draw a conclusion from the foregoing points which will tie the theme of this section to those of previous chapters. My conclusion is this: The logical oddness of the term "I" calls attention to the reality of tacit knowledge with respect to a person's awareness of himself as a self. This conclusion seems to me to be in harmony with, if not implied by, the analyses given by Wittgenstein, Ryle, and Strawson. Wittgenstein spoke of "my own relation to my words. . .[being] wholly different from other people's" in such a way as to tie in with his ruminations about solipsism and "what can be shown but not said." This seems to imply, though he never explicitly states it, that, in speaking, a person has an "awareness" of himself which cannot be put into his own talk about himself, but which is reflected "backhandly," as it were, in the logical peculiarities of the term "I."

Professor Ryle also speaks, albeit casually, in a way which implies this conclusion. On his way to dispelling the seeming mystery attendant to the systematic elusiveness of "I," he remarks that a child "discovers the trick of directing higher order acts upon his own lower order acts." I would like to suggest that what takes place when a child learns to describe his own actions is much more significant and far-reaching than simply learning a trick, or technique. Learning how to use the term "I" is an important and rather high-level activity which reflects a self-awareness that cannot be made fully explicit. Incidentally, there is an important relation between this self-knowledge and the logic of "I" on the one hand, and what Ryle says earlier on in his book about "knowing how" on the other hand. "Knowing how to go on" in the use of "I" provides an important criterion for personal identity.

It is also true that Professor Strawson's account of the relation between "I" and the logical primitiveness of the concept of a person is another way of stating my conclusion that the logical peculiarities of "I" call attention to our tacit knowledge of our own selves. He certainly implies the necessity and reality of such self-knowledge when he maintains that our knowledge of ourselves is not obtained, as in the case of our knowledge of other persons, by means of observation. This is clearly true when one focuses, as he does, upon our "intentional acts." Indeed, it might be added that this is especially true with respect to the act of speaking or the act of using the term "I" in the subject, or higher order, sense.

Just how does the logic of "I" cali attention to a form of tacit knowledge? Well, to begin with, it should be clear that it is not the sort of knowledge which can be made explicit in language. This is not to say that it cannot be talked about at all, but that it can never be put into straightforward behavior-talk in a way that is fully satisfactory. It should not be necessary to repeat the full case against the position which maintains that only what can be made explicit qualifies as knowledge. This position, exemplified in the early writings of Wittgenstein, is implicitly refuted by the fact that he himself managed to say a number of interesting and important things about "what cannot be said clearly." Further, it is explicitly refuted by the work of the later Wittgenstein, as I have argued in Part Two of this book.

To speak of the logic of "I" as calling attention to a form of knowledge which cannot be made fully explicit does not give license for all sorts of foggy talk. There is still a difference, however vague and flexible, between discourse which is significant and discourse which is not. What I have been maintaining is that the peculiar logic of the term "I" points up a form of knowledge which, although it cannot be isolated explicitly, can be seen to play an important role in human experience, thought, and language. Moreover, it is possible to talk about such knowledge, but only indirectly.

In the final analysis, all that can be done when trying to talk about a form of knowledge which by definition cannot be captured in explicit language is to call attention to situations in which such knowledge is "known." Some things cannot be said, but can be seen: ". . .don't think, *look* and see." All that can be done is to ask the reader to reflect on such ethical and existential situations as promise-making and death. Such reflection should make him aware that he knows himself in a way which is both unique and inexplicable.

As our explication of Michael Polanyi's thought in Chapter Five indicated, the clearest case of such tacit knowledge is to be seen in what is often termed "knowing how." Obviously in the area of motor skills we all know how to do things, like riding a bicycle, even though we find it impossible to put this knowledge into words. Such knowledge is a function of high-level coordination between our sensory awareness and our mental-bodily activity. On a much more complex level, our knowledge of other persons is mediated to us by means of their behavior, but obviously cannot be reduced to an account of their behavior. We do, in fact, speak of "knowing" other persons in ways which are not reducible to either or both of the usual disjuncts, "knowing how" and "knowing that." Now it is precisely this sort of knowledge about our own person which is reflected, however indirectly, in the peculiarities of "I."

The whole point is put powerfully in the following quotation from Arthur Koestler's novel, *Darkness at Noon*:

> Rubashov tried to study his newly discovered entity very thoroughly during his wanderings through the cell; with the shyness of emphasizing the first person singular customary in the party, he had christened it the "grammatical fiction." He probably had only a few weeks left to live, and he felt a compelling urge to clear up this matter, to "think it to a logical conclusion." But the realm of the "grammatical fiction" seemed to begin just where the "thinking to a conclusion" ended. It was obviously an essential part of its being, to remain out of the reach of logical thought, and then to take one unawares, as from ambush, and attack one with daydreams and toothache.[25]

I conclude this analysis of "I" with a brief disclaimer. In the foregoing discussion I have not been opting for the existence of a spiritual self, nor for some form of "privileged access" in the introspective sense. Although the self-awareness for which I have been arguing is of top-level importance, both linguistically and experientially, there is nothing "spooky" about it. Intentional acts, and especially the act of using the term "I" in the subject, or elusive, sense, involve a form of self-knowledge which cannot be assimilated either to straightforward observation-talk, or to talk about metaphysical substance. "I am I" is certainly a tautology, but it is, in Ryle's words, a "tautology well worth remembering"!

It now remains to draw out the parallels between the function of the term "I" and that of the term "God." The main parallel is, of course, an asymmetrical one. Whereas "I" has both an object-use and a subject-use, "God" has only what is best termed a "subject-use." This is not to imply that persons use "God" to refer to themselves; it is rather to imply that there is no object-use of "God" in the sense of our being able to substitute object-language terms for it. "God" has a subject-use in the sense that it cannot be reduced to terms pertaining to physical reality. There is a temptation to conclude that the subject-use of "God" is superfluous, since it serves no empirical function. This is simply another way of maintaining that God-talk is meaningless. I trust that the foregoing analysis has made it clear that the subject-use of "I" is far from superfluous. Similarly, one need not conclude that the term "God" is superfluous simply because it is not exchangeable for straightforwardly empirical terms. Although what the religious person seeks to designate by his use of "God" cannot be isolated from the other aspects of experience, it is neither superfluous nor meaningless. God-awareness, like self-awareness, is mediated through other forms of awareness without being reducible to them. Thus God-talk, like I-talk, is related to other kinds of talk, but is not reducible to them.

Another parallel between the terms "I" and "God" pertains to their quasi-naming function. As I pointed out a few pages back, the term "I" can be said to function as a name in that it serves to call attention to the personal identity that holds a person's talk about himself together. In the same way, "God" can be said to function as a name in the sense that it is used to seek to identify an aspect of the religious dimension of experience. The sense in which these two terms are not to be construed as names is brought out in the preceding paragraph. To put this point somewhat differently, there is a sense in which "God," like "person" or "I," has a referential (naming) meaning which is logically primitive in nature; it is not subject to further analysis or empirical identification, but is grasped tacitly by those who find themselves experiencing a dimension of reality with reference to which God-talk emerges as appropriate.

The third parallel between these two terms lies in their common basis in tacit knowledge. The essential but non-reducible character of "I"-logic points up the tacit nature of self-knowledge. Similarly, the essential but nonreducible character of "God"-logic for the religious person points up the tacit structure of religious knowledge. In each case the experiential awareness which gives rise to these unique locutions is mediated in character, and this necessitates an epistemological basis which is tacit in structure. Knowing God, like knowing oneself, is an awareness-activity which can never be made fully explicit. Thus God-talk and I-talk exist on the threshold between tacit and explicit knowledge. Although one must seek to be as articulate as possible about such knowledge (mysticism to the contrary notwithstanding), its most basic aspects can never be made explicit (positivism to the contrary notwithstanding). To borrow a phrase but not a position from the early Wittgenstein, some things that we know "cannot be said, but they can be shown." Tacit knowledge displays itself in the structure of our language and behavior. To quote Ian Ramsey again:

> So our conclusion is that for the religious man "God" is a key word, an irreducible posit, an ultimate of explanation expressive of the kind of *commitment* he professes. It is to be talked about in terms of the object-language over which it presides, but only when this object-language is qualified; in which case this qualified object-language becomes also currency for that odd *discernment* with which religious *commitment*, when it is not bigotry or fanaticism, will necessarily be associated.[26]

One final parallel bears mentioning. Although it was not discussed in the foregoing analysis, it is important to keep in mind that "I" and its correlates, such as "self" and "person," serve an important theoretical function as well as an everyday one. These terms provide the key concepts around which the human sciences from history through sociology to psychology are organized. Thus these terms, when properly qualified, may well provide the key concepts for a chastened, or "descriptive" metaphysics (Strawson's term). In a parallel fashion, the term "God" may be developed in such a way as to serve as an "integrator term" for the overall mapping and interrelating of the various theoretical disciplines. If metaphysics can be viewed as a linguistic activity having as its purpose the integration of the languages of the various sciences into an overall conceptual map, then theology might be construed as a particular alternative metaphysical activity. The religious person is convinced that the language-game known as "theism" provides the best overall conceptual map. Ramsey concludes his analysis of the integrative function of theology by noting the parallel between God-talk and I-talk:

> The possibility of a metaphysical theology arises when, to talk of the objective constituent of all disclosure situations which go beyond what is seen, to unite the various metaphysical words that are cast up in this way, we use the word "God." This word "God" is modelled on, though it has necessarily important differences from, "I." These differences are in fact grounded in the observable features of those various disclosure situations which more aptly lead us to God rather than to ourselves or other people.[27]

These then are the major parallels between God-talk and I-talk. My contention in this section has been that the former is more clearly understood when modeled on the latter. The overall theme of this concluding chapter has been that when theological language is understood in terms of metaphors and models it is no longer necessary to conclude that its logical oddness renders it meaningless. Moreover, the thrust of these two final chapters taken together as Part Three has been to show that it is possible to view religious knowledge and language in a way which is in harmony with the interpretation of knowledge as tacit. Thus the present book is brought to a close. The problem has been located and defined, the solution has been offered and substantiated, and the implications have been sketched out. I conclude that religious knowledge is possible.

Bibliography

Adler, Irving. *Thinking Machines.* New York: New American Library, 1961.

Anscombe, G. E. M. *An Introduction to Wittgenstein's Tractatus.* New York: Harper, 1965.

Austin, J. L. *How To Do Things With Words.* Cambridge: Harvard University Press, 1962.

—————. *Philosophical Papers.* London: Oxford University Press, 1961.

Baier, Kurt. *The Moral Point of View.* New York: Harper, 1961.

Barth, Karl. *Church Dogmatics.* Edinburgh: T. and T. Clark, 1936.

Black, Max. *Models and Metaphors.* Ithaca: Cornell University Press, 1962.

—————. "The Gap Between 'Is' and 'Should'," *The Philosophical Review,* LXXIII, No. 2, April 1964.

Bouillard, Henri. *The Logic of the Faith.* New York: Sheed and Ward, 1967.

Bultmann, Rudolph. *Jesus Christ and Mythology.* New York: Scribners, 1958.

—————. *Kerygma and Myth.* New York: Harper, 1961.

Comte, Auguste. *Positive Philosophy,* trans. by H. Martineau. New York: Calvin Blanchard, 1856.

Edwards, Paul. "Professor Tillich's Confusions," *Mind,* LXXIV, No. 294, April 1965.

Feuerbach, Ludwig. *The Essence of Christianity.* New York: Harper, 1957.

Frankena, W. K. "On Saying the Ethical Thing," *Proceedings and Addresses of the American Philosophical Association,* XXXIX, 1966.

Gill, Jerry. "Kant, Kierkegaard and Religious Knowledge," *Philosophy and Phenomenological Research,* December 1967.

—————. "On 'I'," *Mind,* April 1970.

—————. "The Language of Theology," *Encounter,* XXVII, No. 3, Summer 1967.

————. "The Talk Circle," *Christian Scholar,* Winter 1965.

————. "Wittgenstein's Concept of Truth," *The International Philosophical Quarterly,* VI, No. 1, March 1966.

————. "Wittgenstein on the Use of 'I'," *The Southern Journal of Philosophy,* V, No. 1, Spring 1967.

Hartnack, Justus. *Wittgenstein and Modern Philosophy.* New York: New York University Press, 1965.

Hayakawa, S. I. *Language and Thought in Action.* New York: Harcourt, Brace and World, 1964.

Hegel, G. W. F. *Hegel Selections,* ed. by J. Loewenberg. New York: Scribners, 1929.

Heidegger, Martin. *Existence and Being.* Chicago: Regnery, 1949.

Hick, John. *Faith and Knowledge.* Ithaca: Cornell University Press, 1957.

Holmer, Paul. "Language and Theology," *Harvard Theological Review,* July 1965.

Hordern, William. *Speaking of God.* New York: Macmillan, 1964.

————. *The Case for a New Reformation Theology.* Philadelphia: Westminster, 1959.

Hume, David. *An Inquiry Concerning Human Understanding,* from *The Empiricists,* Section IV, Part 5. Garden City: Doubleday, 1961.

————. *A Treatise of Human Nature.* Garden City: Doubleday, 1961.

Jordan, Robert. "To Tell The Truth," *The Christian Scholar,* LXXIV, No. 4, Winter 1964.

Kant, Immanuel. *Critique of Practical Reason,* trans. by T. K. Abbott in *Great Books of the Western World.* Chicago: Encyclopedia Britannica, Inc., 1951.

————. *Critique of Pure Reason,* trans. by N. K. Smith. New York: St. Martin's Press, 1965.

————. *Prolegomena to Any Future Metaphysics,* trans. by Lewis Beck. New York: The Liberal Arts Press, 1951.

————. *Religion Within the Limits of Reason Alone,* trans. by T. H. Green and H. H. Hudson. New York: Harper, 1960.

Kaufmann, Walter, ed. *Existentialism from Dostoevsky to Sartre.* New York: Meridian, 1956.

Kierkegaard, Søren. *Concluding Unscientific Postscript,* trans. by Walter Lowrie. Princeton: Princeton University Press, 1941.

————. *Philosophical Fragments,* trans. by Walter Lowrie. Princeton: Princeton University Press, 1962.

Koestler, Arthur. *Darkness at Noon.* New York: New American Library, 1948.

————. *Insight and Outlook.* New York: Macmillan, 1949.

————. *The Act of Creation.* New York: Macmillan, 1964.

Kraft, Victor. *The Vienna Circle*. New York: The Philosophical Library, 1953.

Mackenzie, P. T. "Fact and Value," *Mind*, LXXVI, No. 302, April 1967.

Merleau-Ponty, Maurice. *Phenomenology of Perception*, trans. by Colin Smith. London: Routledge and Kegan Paul, 1962.

Novak, Michael. *Belief and Unbelief*. New York: Macmillan, 1965.

Ortega y Gasset, Jose. *Man and People*. New York: Norton, 1957.

Pannenberg, Wolfhart. "The Revelation of God in Jesus of Nazareth," *Theology as History*, Vol. III in *New Frontiers in Theology*, ed. by James M. Robinson and John B. Cobb, Jr. New York: Harper, 1967.

Pasch, Alan. *Experience and the Analytic*. Chicago: University of Chicago Press, 1958.

Pitcher, George. *The Philosophy of Wittgenstein*. Englewood Cliffs: Prentice-Hall, 1964.

Plato. *The Republic*, trans. by F. M. Cornford. New York: Oxford, 1945.

Polanyi, Michael. *Personal Knowledge*. New York: Harper, 1964.

—————. "The Logic of Tacit Inference," *Philosophy*, XLI, October 1918-July 1919.

—————. *The Tacit Dimension*. Garden City: Doubleday, 1966.

Poteat, William. "God and the Private-I," *Philosophy and Phenomenological Research*, March 1960.

Ramsey, Ian. "Ethics and Reason," *The Church Quarterly Review*, CLVIII, April-June 1957.

—————. *Models and Mystery*. New York: Oxford University Press, 1964.

—————. *Prospect for Metaphysics*. New York: The Philosophical Library, 1961.

—————. "Religion and Science: A Philosopher's Approach," *The Church Quarterly Review*, CLXII, January-March 1961.

—————. *Religious Language*. New York: Macmillan, 1955.

—————. "Talking About God: Models, Ancient, and Modern," *Myth and Symbol*, ed. by F. W. Dillistone. London: SPCK Press, 1966.

—————. "The Logical Character of Resurrection-belief," *Theology*, LX, No. 433, May 1957.

—————. "The Systematic Elusiveness of 'I'," *Philosophical Quarterly*, January 1959.

—————. "Towards the Relevant in Theological Language," *The Modern Churchman*, VIII, September 1964.

Reichenbach, Hans. *The Rise of Scientific Philosophy*. Berkeley: University of California Press, 1958.

Robinson, J. M. *A New Quest for the Historical Jesus.* London: SCM Press, 1959.

Russell, Bertrand. "Philosophy of Logical Atomism," *The Monist*, V, October 1918-July 1919.

Ryle, Gilbert. *The Concept of Mind.* New York: Barnes and Noble, 1949.

Schleiermacher, Friedrich. *The Christian Faith.* New York: Harper, 1963.

Searle, J. R. "How to Derive 'Ought' from 'Is'," *The Philosophical Review*, LXXIII, No. 1, January 1964.

Smith, J. E. *Reason and God.* New Haven: Yale University Press, 1961.

Strawson, P. F. *Individuals.* London: Methuen, 1959.

————. "Persons," *The Philosophy of Mind*, ed. by V. C. Chappell. Englewood Cliffs: Prentice-Hall, 1962.

————. *The Bounds of Sense.* London: Methuen, 1966.

Stroud, Barry. "Wittgenstein's Logical Necessity," *Philosophical Review*, LXXIV, No. 4, October 1965.

Thomas, G. F. *Religious Philosophies of the West.* New York: Scribners, 1965.

Tillich, Paul. *Dynamics of Faith.* New York: Harper, 1957.

————. *Systematic Theology*, Vol. I. Chicago: University of Chicago Press, 1951.

Toulmin, Stephen. *An Examination of the Place of Reason in Ethics.* Cambridge: Cambridge University Press, 1950.

Turbayne, C. M. *The Myth of Metaphor.* New Haven: Yale University Press, 1962.

Walters, Carl. "Where the Action Is," *Theology Today*, XXIV, No. 2, July 1967.

Wisdom, John. *Paradox and Discovery.* Oxford: Blackwell, 1965.

————. *Philosophy and Psychoanalysis.* Oxford: Blackwell, 1953.

Wittgenstein, Ludwig. *The Blue and Brown Books.* New York: Harper, 1960.

————. "Lecture on Ethics," *The Philosophical Review*, LXXIV, No. 1, January 1956.

————. *Philosophical Investigations.* New York: Macmillan, 1953.

————. *Tractatus Logico-Philosophicus*, trans. by D. F. Pears and B. F. McGuinness. London: Routledge and Kegan Paul, 1961.

Notes

Chapter I

[1] *Existentialism from Dostoevsky to Sartre* (New York: Meridian, 1956), p. 51.

[2] "A Lecture on Ethics," *The Philosophical Review,* LXXIV, No. 1 (Jan. 1965), 6.

[3] *Ibid.,* pp. 7, 8.

[4] *Ibid.,* p. 10.

[5] *Ibid.,* pp. 8, 9.

[6] *The Rise of Scientific Philosophy* (Berkeley: University of California Press, 1958), p. 277.

[7] *Ibid.,* p. 282.

[8] "Professor Tillich's Confusions," *Mind,* LXXIV, No. 294 (April 1965).

[9] *Ibid.,* pp. 199-200.

[10] Parts of this summary of Heidegger are taken from my article entitled "The Language of Theology," *Encounter,* XXVII, No. 3 (Summer 1966).

[11] "What is Metaphysics?" *Existence and Being* (Chicago: Regnery, 1949), pp. 270-291.

[12] *Existentialism from Dostoevsky to Sartre,* pp. 206-221.

[13] Heidegger, "Hölderlin and the Essence of Poetry," *Existence and Being,* p. 283.

[14] Published in *Philosophy and Religion: Some Contemporary Perspectives,* ed. Jerry H. Gill (Minneapolis: Burgess Publishing Co., 1968).

[15] *Ibid.,* p. 62.

[16] *Ibid.,* p. 12.

[17] *Man and People* (New York: Norton, 1957), p. 17.

[18] *Ibid.,* p. 101.

[19] "Existentialism is a Humanism," *Existentialism from Dostoevsky to Sartre,* p. 297.

[20] The following summary of Kierkegaard's position is adapted from my article "Kant, Kierkegaard and Religious Knowledge," *Philosophy and Phenomenological Research,* Dec. 1967.

21 Volume VII (1846), A, 186 (Princeton: Princeton University Press, 1941), p. xv.

22 *Philosophical Fragments* (Princeton: Princeton University Press, 1962), pp. 16ff.

23 *Ibid.*, p. 72.

24 *Ibid.*, p. 59.

25 *Ibid.*, p. 72.

26 *Ibid.*, p. 76.

27 *Ibid.*, p. 108.

28 *Ibid.*, p. 130.

29 *Concluding Unscientific Postscript*, p. 31.

30 *Ibid.*, p. 55.

31 *Ibid.*, p. 61.

32 *Ibid.*, p. 109.

33 Karl Barth, *Church Dogmatics* (Edinburgh: T. and T. Clark, 1936), Vol. I, Part I, p. 245.

34 *Ibid.*, p. 222.

35 *The Case for a New Reformation Theology* (Philadelphia: Westminster, 1959), p. 74.

36 The dichotomous nature of Hordern's position is also reflected in his book dealing with the problem of the meaning of religious language, *Speaking of God* (New York: Macmillan, 1964). For a critique of Hordern's book, see my review, "The Talk Circle," in *The Christian Scholar* (Winter 1965).

37 *The Case for a New Reformation Theology*, p. 93.

38 *Kerygma and Myth* (New York: Harper, 1961), p. 10.

39 *Jesus Christ and Mythology* (New York: Scribners, 1958), p. 84.

40 *Dynamics of Faith* (New York: Harper, 1957), pp. 96-97.

41 *Systematic Theology*, Vol. I (Chicago: University of Chicago, 1951), p. 238.

Chapter II

1 G.W.F. Hegel, "Introduction to the Philosphy of History," *Hegel Selections*, ed. J. Loewenberg (New York: Scribners, 1929), pp. 348-49.

2 *Ibid.*, esp. pp. 358-369; 386-89.

3 *Ibid.*, "The Philosophy of Mind" (Section Two), pp. 218ff.

4 *Ibid.*, "Phenomenology of Mind" (Preface), p. 16. In speaking of his system, Hegel also says that it is "a view which the developed exposition of. . .can alone justify" (p. 14).

5 *Ibid.*, p. 20.

6 *Ibid.*, p. 14.

7 *Ibid.*, p. 15.

8 *Ibid.*, pp. 104 ff.

[9] *Ibid.*, pp. 18-19.

[10] *Ibid.*, "The Philosophy of History," p. 385.

[11] *Ibid.*, p. 355.

[12] *Ibid.*, p. 356.

[13] *The Christian Faith* (New York: Harper, 1963), Vol. I, p. 5.

[14] *Ibid.*, p. 7.

[15] *Ibid.*, p. 11.

[16] *Ibid.*, p. 12 (No. 4).

[17] *Ibid.*, p. 13.

[18] *Ibid.*

[19] *Ibid.*, p. 16.

[20] *Ibid.*, pp. 77-93 (No. 15-19).

[21] *Ibid.*, especially pp. 194 ff. (No. 50).

[22] *The Essence of Christianity* (New York: Harper, 1957), p. 3.

[23] *Ibid.*, p. 6.

[24] *Ibid.*, p. 11.

[25] *Ibid.*

[26] *Ibid.*, p. 12.

[27] *Ibid.*, p. 15.

[28] *Ibid.*, p. 14.

[29] *Ibid.*, p. 17.

[30] *Ibid.*, p. 29.

[31] *Ibid.*, p. 46.

[32] *Ibid.*, p. 57.

[33] *Ibid.*, p. 184.

[34] *Ibid.*, p. xxxix.

[35] Auguste Comte, *Positive Philosophy*, trans. H. Martineau (New York: Calvin Blanchard, 1856), p. 26.

Chapter III

[1] *The Republic*, trans. F. M. Cornford (New York: Oxford, 1945), Book X, 604, pp. 336-37.

[2] *An Enquiry Concerning Human Understanding*, Section IV, Part I, from *The Empiricists* (Garden City: Doubleday, 1961), p. 322.

[3] *Ibid.*, Section XII, Part III, p. 430.

[4] *A Treatise of Human Nature*, Book III, Part I, Section I, quoted from the Doubleday edition, 1961, p. 422.

[5] The following discussion of Kant's position is adapted from my article "Kant, Kierkegaard, and Religious Knowledge," *Philosophy and Phenomenological Research*, Dec. 1967.

[6] *Critique of Pure Reason*, trans. Norman Kemp Smith (New York: St. Martin's Press, 1965), p. 41 (B1).

7 *Ibid.*, pp. 43-54 (B2-18/A3-10); pp. 102-119 (B89-B16/A65-83).

8 *Ibid.*, p. 259 (A239/B299).

9 *Ibid.*, pp. 327-484 (A339-567/B397-595).

10 *Prolegomena to Any Future Metaphysics,* trans. Lewis Beck (New York: The Liberal Arts Press, 1951), pp. 80-98 (Sections 45-56).

11 *Pure Reason,* p. 528 (A636/B664).

12 *Prolegomena,* p. 114 (Solution).

13 *Critique of Practical Reason,* trans. T.K. Abbott, Vol. XLII of the *Great Books of the Western World* (Chicago: Encyclopedia Britannica, Inc., 1951), p. 292 (Preface).

14 *Ibid.*, p. 296 (Introduction).

15 See *Pure Reason,* p. 530 (A640-B668); *Practical Reason,* pp. 346-47 (Part I, Book II, Chapter II, Section V).

16 *Religion Within the Limits of Reason Alone,* trans. T.H. Green and H.H. Hudson (New York: Harper, 1960), p. 94.

17 *Pure Reason,* p. 531 (A641/B669).

18 *Practical Reason,* p. 353 (Book II, Chapter II, Section VIII).

19 *Pure Reason,* p. 29 (B xxx).

20 *The Bounds of Sense* (London: Methuen, 1966), p. 226.

21 George F. Thomas, *Religious Philosophies of the West* (New York: Scribners, 1965), p. 257.

22 *Reason and God* (New Haven: Yale University Press, 1961), pp. 18-19.

23 *Pure Reason,* p. 257 (A236/B295).

Chapter IV

1 *Belief and Unbelief* (New York: Macmillan, 1965), p. 29.

2 *Language and Thought in Action* (New York: Harcourt, Brace and World, 1964).

3 Irving Adler, *Thinking Machines* (New York: New American Library, 1961), pp. 57-59.

4 "Philosophy of Logical Atomism," *The Monist,* V (Oct. 1918 through July 1919).

5 *Tractatus Logico-Philosophicus,* trans. D.F. Pears and B.F. McGuinness (London: Routledge and Kegan Paul, 1961).

6 *Ibid.*, p. 7 (1, 1.1).

7 *Ibid.*, p. 23 (3.203, 3.22).

8 *Ibid.*, p. 43 (4.0311-2).

9 *Ibid.*, p. 19 (2.221-3).

10 See G.E.M. Anscombe, *An Introduction to Wittgenstein's Tractatus* (New York: Harper, 1956), pp. 150 ff.

11 For an excellent account of this group, see Victor Kraft's *The Vienna Circle* (New York: The Philosophical Library, 1953).

12 *Pure Reason,* p. 65 (A19/B33).

[13] *Tractatus,* p. 3 (Preface).

[14] *Philosophical Investigations* (New York: Macmillan, 1953), p. 155 (No. 593).

[15] *Ibid.,* p. 11 (No. 23).

[16] *Ibid.,* p. 13 (No. 27).

[17] *Ibid.,* p. 109 (No. 340).

[18] *Ibid.,* cf. pp. 6 (No. 11) and 47 (No. 108) respectively.

[19] *Ibid.,* p. 7 (No. 12).

[20] For a more thorough discussion of these matters, the reader may turn to George Pitcher's *The Philosophy of Wittgenstein* (Englewood Cliffs: Prentice-Hall, 1964), and Justus Hartnack's *Wittgenstein and Modern Philosophy* (New York: New York University Press, 1965).

[21] *Investigations,* p. 46 (No. 107).

[22] *Ibid.,* pp. 138-39 (No. 499).

[23] *Ibid.,* p. 33 (No. 70).

[24] *Ibid.,* p. 27 (No. 54).

[25] *Ibid.,* p. 11 (No. 23).

[26] *Ibid.,* p. 226.

[27] *Ibid.,* p. 85 (No. 217).

[28] For a full defense of this interpretation, see Barry Stroud's "Wittgenstein and Logical Necessity," *Philosophical Review,* LXXIV, No. 4 (Oct. 1965).

[29] I have in mind such facts as these: 1) no matter how primitive a people, their language is always highly developed and complex; 2) Helen Keller, a blind deaf-mute, insists that before learning to use language she was not really a person, but only a "phantom" who never performed an intentional act.

[30] *Investigations,* p. 88 (No. 241-42).

[31] It must be acknowledged, to be sure, that the tolerance principle has often been exploited by those who have sought to sidestep the challenge of logical empiricism to the religious use of language. For examples of this tendency, the reader may refer to William Hordern's *Speaking of God* (New York: Macmillan, 1964) and Paul Holmer's "Language and Theology," *Harvard Theological Review,* July 1965. Wittgenstein did not maintain that just because a certain way of speaking can be said to exist, it is *ipso facto* a meaningful way of speaking. On the contrary, language-games exist in overlapping, criss-crossing relationship to one another, and consequently are to some degree "answerable" to one another. Furthermore, any given use of language must be grounded in an experiential "form of life" which is participated in by a substantial number of persons.

[32] *Paradox and Discovery* (Oxford: Blackwell, 1965), p. ix (Introduction).

[33] Strawson uses the phrase in reference to the concept "person" in his book *Individuals* (London: Methuen, 1959).

[34] *Philosophical Papers* (London: Oxford University Press, 1961), p. 222.

[35] *Ibid.,* pp. 224, 238.

[36] *How To Do Things With Words* (Cambridge: Harvard University Press, 1962), pp. 90-93.

[37] *Ibid.*, pp. 98-107.

[38] Austin says as much on page 146 of *How To Do Things With Words* when he states: "...the locutionary act as much as the illocutionary is an abstraction only: every genuine speech-act is both."

[39] *Ibid.*, p. 141.

[40] *Ibid.*, pp. 141-42.

[41] *Ibid.*, p. 152.

[42] *Ibid.*, pp. 147-48.

[43] That this interpretation is in line with Austin's overall position can be seen by examining his analyses of the terms "truth" and "knowledge" in *Philosophical Papers,* pp. 85-101 and pp. 44-84 respectively.

[44] *Models and Metaphors* (Ithaca: Cornell University Press, 1962), p. 46.

Chapter V

[1] One brief quotation from Tillich makes this point explicit: "Science has no right and no power to interfere with faith and faith has no power to interfere with science. One dimension of meaning is not able to interfere with another dimension" (*Dynamics of Faith,* pp. 81-82).

[2] I should here acknowledge my debt to John Hick's development of the concept of dimensions in his excellent book *Faith and Knowledge* (Ithaca: Cornell University Press, 1957), Chapter Six. I will explain his position more fully in Chapter Seven.

[3] *Phenomenology of Perception,* trans. Colin Smith (London: Routledge and Kegan Paul, 1962).

[4] Some have even questioned the meaningfulness of such questioning. See Stephen Toulmin's *An Examination of the Place of Reason in Ethics* (Cambridge: Cambridge University Press, 1950) and Kurt Baier's *The Moral Point of View* (New York: Random House, 1965).

[5] *Belief and Unbelief,* p. 83.

[6] *Philosophical Investigations,* p. 190. For a further analysis see my "Wittgenstein on the Use of 'I'," *The Southern Journal of Philosophy,* V, No. 1 (Spring 1967).

[7] New York: Dover Publications, 1952.

[8] *Experience and the Analytic* (Chicago: University of Chicago Press, 1958), p. 202.

[9] *Ibid.,* pp. 212-240.

[10] *Ibid.,* pp. 209-210.

[11] See especially Chapters Four ("Skills") and Five ("Articulation") of his *Personal Knowledge* (New York: Harper, 1964); also Chapter One of *The Tacit Dimension* (Garden City: Doubleday, 1966).

[12] *Personal Knowledge,* p. x (Preface).

[13] *Ibid.,* p. x (Preface).

[14] *The Tacit Dimension,* p. 22.

[15] "The Logic of Tacit Inference," *Philosophy,* XLI (Jan. 1966), p. 14.

Chapter VI

[1] *Belief and Unbelief,* pp. 97-98.

[2] *Philosophical Papers,* p. 67.

[3] *Personal Knowledge,* p. 309.

[4] "Fact and Value," *Mind,* LXXVI, No. 302 (April 1967).

[5] *Ibid.,* p. 228.

[6] *Ibid.,* p. 237.

[7] "On Saying the Ethical Thing," *Proceedings and Addresses of the American Philosophical Association,* XXIX (1966).

[8] Max Black, "The Gap Between 'Is' and 'Should'," *The Philosophical Review,* LXXIII, No. 2 (April 1964); John R. Searle, "How to Derive 'Ought' from 'Is'," *The Philosophical Review,* LXXIII, No. 1 (Jan. 1964).

[9] *Philosophical Papers,* p. 95.

[10] *Ibid.,* p. 98.

[11] Parts of this analysis were first published in *The International Philosophical Quarterly,* VI, No. 1 (March 1966) under the title "Wittgenstein's Concept of Truth."

[12] *Investigations,* p. 52 (No. 136).

[13] *Ibid.,* p. 88 (No. 241-42).

[14] *Ibid.,* p. 223.

[15] *Ibid.,* p. 227.

[16] *Ibid.,* p. 228.

[17] *Ibid.*

[18] *Ibid.*

[19] *Ibid.,* p. 229.

[20] *Ibid.,* p. 228.

[21] *The Christian Scholar,* XLVII, No. 4 (Winter 1964), p. 309.

[22] *Ibid.*

[23] For a helpful account of this concept, see Pasch's *Experience and the Analytic,* pp. 255-265.

[24] For a full-scale criticism of this view, consult C.M. Turbayne's *The Myth of Metaphor* (New Haven: Yale University Press, 1962).

[25] *Models and Metaphors,* pp. 30-37. For another helpful account of the cognitivity of metaphor, see Arthur Koestler's *The Act of Creation* (New York: Macmillan, 1964), and his *Insight and Outlook* (New York: Macmillan, 1949).

[26] *Models and Metaphors,* p. 44.

[27] *Ibid.,* p. 46.

[28] *Ibid.,* pp. 219-231.

29 *Ibid.*, p. 229.

30 *Ibid.*

31 *Ibid.*, p. 238.

Chapter VII

1 *Faith and Knowledge* (Ithaca: Cornell University Press, 1957), p. 110.

2 *Ibid.*, pp. 121-22.

3 *Ibid.*, pp. 127, 129.

4 *Ibid.*, p. 172.

5 *Ibid.*, pp. 196-97.

6 The main lines of the above account are common knowledge, but the reader may wish to consult the excellent summary of the issue in James M. Robinson's *A New Quest for the Historical Jesus* (London: SCM Press, 1959). See also *Theology as History*, Volume III in *New Frontiers in Theology*, ed. James M. Robinson and John B. Cobb, Jr. (New York: Harper, 1967).

7 *The Logic of Faith* (New York: Sheed and Ward, 1967), p. 17.

8 See *The New Hermeneutic*, Vol. II of *New Frontiers in Theology* (New York: Harper, 1964).

9 See especially pages 125-131.

10 "The Revelation of God in Jesus," the focal essay in *Theology as History*, p. 118.

11 Ian T. Ramsey, *Religious Language* (New York: Macmillan, 1955), pp. 25-26.

12 *Philosophical Investigations*, pp. 193-214.

13 *Religious Language*, pp. 35-36.

14 *Ibid.*, pp. 78-79.

15 "Religion and Science: A Philosopher's Approach," *The Church Quarterly Review*, CLXII (Jan.-March, 1961), pp. 77 ff.

16 "Ethics and Reason," *The Church Quarterly Review*, CLVIII (April-June 1957), pp. 153 ff.

17 "On the Possibility and Purpose of a Metaphysical Theology," *Prospect for Metaphysics* (New York: The Philosophical Library, 1961).

18 *Religious Language*, pp. 17-18.

19 Gilbert Ryle, *The Concept of Mind* (New York: Barnes and Noble, 1949), and P.F. Strawson, "Persons," *The Philosophy of Mind,* ed. V.C. Chappell (Englewood Cliffs: Prentice-Hall, 1962), Chapter VII. Wittgenstein says something similar to this in his *Philosophical Investigations*, p. 178.

20 *Prospect for Metaphysics*, pp. 169-170.

21 "Towards the Relevant in Theological Language," *The Modern Churchman,* VIII (Sept. 1964), p. 50.

22 "Talking About God: Models, Ancient, and Modern," *Myth and Symbol,* ed. F. W. Dillistone (London: SPCK Press, 1966), p. 87.

23 *Religious Language*, p. 39.

[24] *Ibid.*, p. 53.

[25] "The Logical Character of Resurrection-belief," *Theology*, LX, No. 443 (May 1957), p. 192.

[26] *Models and Mystery* (New York: Oxford University Press, 1964), p. 38.

[27] "Where the Action Is," *Theology Today*, XXIV, No. 2 (July 1967), p. 207.

Chapter VIII

[1] *Paradox and Discovery*, p. 7.

[2] *Ibid.*, pp. 3-4.

[3] *Ibid.*, p. 132.

[4] *Ibid.*, p. 101. See also Chapter Six, "The Metamorphosis of Metaphysics," pp. 57-81.

[5] *Ibid.*, p. 124. See also Chapter One, "The Logic of God," pp. 1-22.

[6] *Found in Philosophy and Psychoanalysis* (Oxford: Blackwell, 1953).

[7] *Religious Language*, pp. 59-60.

[8] *Ibid.*, pp. 69ff.

[9] *Ibid.*, pp. 198-99.

[10] *Belief and Unbelief*, p. 116.

[11] The following discussion of the term "I" is adapted from my article "On 'I'," in *Mind*, April 1970.

[12] *The Blue and Brown Books* (New York: Harper, 1960), pp. 64-71.

[13] *Philosophical Investigations*, pp. 122-23 (No. 404-410).

[14] *Ibid.*, pp. 190-92, Section X.

[15] *Ibid.*, p. 190.

[16] *Ibid.*, p. 192. For a more detailed analysis of Wittgenstein's thoughts on "I," see my "Wittgenstein on the Use of 'I'," *The Southern Journal of Philosophy*, No. 1 (Spring 1967).

[17] *The Concept of Mind*, pp. 195-98.

[18] *Ibid.*, p. 193.

[19] *Ibid.*, p. 198.

[20] *Individuals* (London: Methuen, 1959), p. 99.

[21] *Ibid.*, pp. 101-03. This concept was discussed in Section Two of Chapter Four in the present book.

[22] *Ibid.*, p. 103.

[23] Here I am indebted to Ian Ramsey's "The Systematic Elusiveness of 'I'," *Philosophical Quarterly*, July 1955.

[24] These points are discussed by William H. Poteat in "I Will Die: An Analysis," *Philosophical Quarterly*, Jan. 1959; and "God and the Private-I," *Philosophy and Phenomenological Research*, March 1960.

[25] *Darkness at Noon* (New York: New American Library, 1948), p. 100.

[26] *Religious Language*, p. 53.

[27] *Prospect for Metaphysics*, p. 174.

Index